HOSANNA WONG

SUPER ADDED

A LIFE OF MORE. A LIFE OF ADDITION.
A LIFE ABUNDANT, NO LESS.

Superadded

Published by Hosanna Poetry Ministries, Los Angeles, California in partnership with Design Inspirations, Phoenix, Arizona.

Design by: Lindsey Pruitt / Soul Twin Studio
Content Editor: Stephanie Coats
Copy Editor: Sara Remley
Author Photo by: Stefanie Vinsel
Printed by: Design Inspirations

ISBN: 978-0- 692-09220- 0

Printed in the United States of America
2018—First Edition

TO SEAN, SHELLEY, ALLISON, KATE, AND EMILY

In 2011, you changed my life. Your joy, your integrity, and your fearlessness continue to inspire me. I love you deeply. Thank you for being my superadded family.

ABOUT THIS BOOK

This book has super short chapters with super practical applications.

You can read it alone, with a friend, or with a small group. It's set up well for all of that.

It's 28 chapters, 4 sections, 7 chapters per a section. You could read 1 chapter a day for 4 weeks. Boom.

This is also a great airplane read. Seriously, you could read it in one sitting. Do what's best for you/whatever you love the most.

Enjoy it while drinking your favorite coffee (*or if you hate coffee don't you DARE defile this book by drinking coffee. Drink your favorite tea! Or soda! Or juice box!*)

Read at your favorite park. Read in your living room with your favorite candle burning. Read while eating that one pizza you rarely get because you have to add on extra toppings... add on those toppings!

Super-add onto your reading experience.

I hope these words super-add onto your life.

— *Hosanna*

CONTENTS

PERIS

pe-rēs-so's

περισσός

SSOS

greater, excessive, abundant; [1]
beyond what is anticipated, exceeding expectation;
going past the expected limit, more than enough, [2]
over and above, more than is necessary, and superadded [3]

SUPERADDED

INTRO

Not too long ago, I asked God for a superadded life.

I asked Him for *more.*

I have mourned many losses. I have celebrated many victories.

I have dared many adventures. I've conquered many fears.

And I've been defeated. But I've also been rescued. I've been shown compassion. Over and over again.

And I found myself in my backyard, talking to God about the honest state of my heart.

I was recalling the peaks. I was replaying the canyons. I was repeating the characters. I began to weep as I remembered the places, the people, and the unexplainable moments that brought me to this chair, at this house, in this city, with this life, and I whispered,

You know I'm ready. I know I'm ready. I'm not playing around. I want more.

Give me all that you have for me. Don't hold back.

I want a life abundant, no less. Pour it out. Pile it on. Super-add.

I don't want to miss one thing.

What followed my prayer was a whole *lot* of addition... and, to be honest, some subtraction.

I wanted all He had for me?

Turns out, I had to be rid of the other things that were filling me up—the *less* that I was settling for.

To make room.

To make space.

So that He could…

Fill.

Overflow.

Super-add.

And He did.

My prayer for you as you go through these super short chapters on a super abundant life is that you will want more, ask for more, reach for more, be prepared for more, and have the guts to subtract everything that is less—so that God has all of the space to flood your life with the extraordinary.

He wants to give us so much more.

And we can have it. If we want it.

Get excited.

This is going to be *super*.

PART ONE

CHAPTER 01: SUPERADDED LIFE

Jesus came to give us a life of *more.*

It's taken me some time to realize that.

At some point growing up someone must have taught me that following Jesus was about living without, living with *less*, and living exempt from the things that made me happy, because when I would think about receiving Jesus and living for God my first thought would be, "What will I have to *subtract*?"

Turns out, Jesus is all about addition.

The Bible tells us story after story about a God who is adding, multiplying, blessing, and—dare I say—spoiling His children with gift after gift, joy after joy, good thing after good thing, and desires to give us even more. Jesus explicitly tells us that.

In John 10:10, Jesus says, **"I came that they may have life and have it abundantly."** (ESV)

The MSG translation puts it this way: **"So they can have real and eternal life, more and better life than they ever dreamed of."** (MSG)

Have you heard the term "abundant life?" It comes from this passage. The Greek word used here to express that life is *perissos* (pronounced pe-rēs-so's). This word means *greater, excessive, abundant;*[1] *beyond what is anticipated, exceeding expectation; going past the expected limit, more than enough,*[2] *over and above, more than is necessary, and superadded.*[3]

How cool is it that *superadded* is a real word!? I didn't make it up! It's how Jesus described the life He came to give us. I straight up love this word. I never fully understood this verse when it talks about *abundant life*, but superadded? *I get that.*

It makes me think of when I get frozen yogurt. I flood that sweet icy goodness with massive amounts of toppings. I'm adding an excess of Oreos, cookie dough (*c'mon somebody!*), sprinkles, granola, and strawberries (because I'm *kind of* healthy) and then—right when I think I have enough, just as the candied garnishes begin to overflow out of the cup, as people are turning their heads thinking I have too much—I decide to add some *more.*

More than I need. Above and beyond what it necessary. Superadded.

Jesus' main purpose was to give us a life like *that.* A life that is extremely amazing, over the top and abundant, superadded, with all the excess toppings pouring over, more than we need, past all limitations, with joy we've never dreamed of, with love beyond measure, and *overflowing* with confidence, peace, and goodness that no one else can give us.

Jesus did not come to put limits on our lives. He came for us to have lives exceeding our limits. He came to lavish us with all the additions, all the bonuses, and all the *extra.* He came to super-add. Everything Jesus came to give, teach, and show us, was about us living lives of *more.*

QUESTIONS

WHAT DO YOU THINK OF WHEN YOU HEAR THE WORD "SUPERADDED"?

WHY DO YOU SUPPOSE WE SOMETIMES THINK OF LIVING FOR GOD AS A LIFE OF SUBTRACTION, INSTEAD OF ADDITION?

WHAT DOES IT REVEAL TO YOU OR MEAN TO YOU THAT JESUS CAME TO GIVE US A SUPERADDED LIFE?

PRAYER

I

God, I want to know about this life of *more*.
I want to receive all that you have for me.
I don't want to miss out on one thing.
Show me what it means to live a superadded life.

Amen.

CHAPTER 02: SUPERADDED BEST

WE ARE STILL GETTING BETTER + BETTER...

"I am confident that the Creator, who has begun such a great work among you, will not stop in mid-design but will keep perfecting you until the day Jesus the Anointed, our Liberating King, returns to redeem the world.

Here's what I pray for you:

***Father,* may their love grow more and more in wisdom and insight— so they will be able to *examine and* determine the best *from everything else...*"** Philippians 1:6, 9-10 (VOICE)

(Continued in verse 11)

"...a life Jesus will be proud of." (MSG)

God wants us to have the very best.

He wants us to be our very best selves, to love others our very best, and to live our days our very best.

The writer in Philippians (his name is Paul) acknowledges what we already know: we're not exactly at our very best yet. There are things we still want to be better at. There are perspectives we still want to improve. There are relationships we still want to grow in.

This verse encourages us that God—who has already been at work in our lives since the beginning—is merely in mid-design! None of us yet have all the abundance that God has in store for us. None of us yet have all of the blessings, and lessons, and aha moments that God wants for us. There is *more* to be had.

Paul's prayer is that in this process, in this mid-design moment, that our love would grow in wisdom and experience, and that we would be able to examine, assess, and decisively know **"the best from everything else."**

This verse is not merely talking of "good" and "bad." It's literally saying that there's a superadded best, an absolute and abundant *best*, and then, there's ***"everything else."***

I love that. There is God's best. And then there's the *less*. Maybe it's good, even *really* good. But it's not best. Maybe it feels good. But it's not best. Maybe it gets lots of likes on Instagram. But it's not best. Maybe it's super impressive. But it's not best.

In order for us to receive God's best, we will need the discernment to know what is and, more importantly, what isn't His best. And then we'll need to have the courage to choose His best.

If we want God to add on all He has for us, there will be some things we'll need to subtract.

This super-addition will take some honest reflection and some humbling subtraction.

But this is not so we live our lives with *less*.

Without a doubt, this subtraction is so that there is room for more—room for God's over-the-top and excessive *best*.

We are in mid-design because there are hurts we're still holding onto. There are relationships we're not healed from. There are selfish motives we're not letting go of. There is pride standing in the way of us and the person we truly want to be.

God wants so much more for us. He wants us to grow in wisdom, experience, and discernment, and honestly assess what is His best and what is everything else.

This subtraction may be difficult. But the addition will be the *best.*

QUESTIONS

HOW DOES IT MAKE YOU FEEL KNOWING THAT YOU ARE IN "MID-DESIGN"?

WHAT ARE THINGS IN YOUR LIFE THAT YOU KNOW ARE NOT GOD'S BEST?

WHAT WOULD IT LOOK LIKE TO SUBTRACT THOSE THINGS IN YOUR LIFE?

WHAT WOULD IT LOOK LIKE TO REPLACE THOSE THINGS BY ADDING ON GOD'S BEST?

WHAT WOULD YOUR LIFE LOOK LIKE IF YOU MADE THE DAILY DECISION TO ONLY PURSUE AND ADD ON WHAT WAS BEST?

PRAYER

God, I don't want to settle for anything less than all that You have for me. Thank You that I am only in mid-design. Please help me grow in wisdom. Help me grow in discernment. Help me be better at seeing what is the best—Your best—and what is everything else. I want to subtract everything in my life that is less than what You have for me. I want to make room for You to super-add onto my life.

Amen.

CHAPTER 03: SUPERADDED TEAM

MORE FRIENDS. MORE COMMUNITY. ALL THE TEAMMATES.

Who is on your team?

Who do you fight for?

Who is fighting for you?

One of the biggest additions God wants us to have in our lives is a genuinely great community—a group of fighters and teammates alongside of us—for the hard times and fun times, for the sad moments and the parties.

We see this need in the first human God ever created.

God created the whole world, and with every created bird, fish, planet, and star, **"God saw everything"** and saw that **"it was very good."** Genesis 1:31 (ESV)

It wasn't until He created Adam that He said something different.

"It's not good for the Man to be alone; I'll make him a helper, a companion." Genesis 2:18 (MSG)

This is the first time we read of God saying that something is not good. But sin had not entered the world yet. We're still verses away from that slithering snake tempting Eve to eat that fruit. So even before sin and darkness had their foothold in the world, God already saw something that was not good: man being alone.

Enter: Eve.

This is how much God values companionship, community, and intimate relationships. It was essential to our human existence that we would not be alone.

Psalm 133:1 says, **"How good and pleasant it is when God's people live together in unity!"** (NIV)

It is *not good*, it is not *perissos*, for any of us to be alone. In fact, it is *against* God's design.

It is **"good and pleasant"** (the MSG version says **"wonderful"** and **"beautiful"**) for the people of God to link up, team up, and support each other.

So the question is—how intentional are we being with super-adding God's people into our lives?

How are we going out of our way to invest into other people?

How are we budgeting our money to take trips to see our friends?

If we want a superadded life, community is a main addition we must take seriously, and we must be intentional in.

We all need a great team. We all need people who will carry us when we're down, who will rebuke us when we're wrong, who love us and are loyal to us, and who put up with our crazy selves.

If we are lacking in the team department, my hope is that we would honestly assess how to meet this need. What are ways that we can be braver and more intentional with relationships? Perhaps there's a small group or a book club we could get plugged into, or a handful of people we could reach out to.

If we have a large team, but no-one so close that we can be vulnerable and candid with, how can we take steps towards finding that person? Or maybe we simply need to invest in someone who is already in our circle. A first step might even be just taking a few people out on coffee or lunch dates.

If we have a great team, let us reach out to them and encourage them today. Let them know they are our *superadded*. Tell them all they add onto our lives. May we never let these friendships go stale. Let us look at our calendars and see ways we can go *above and beyond what is necessary* for our team in this season. Also, let us look around our communities. Is there anyone else who may be team-less, or lonely, or lacking in this addition that we already have? Is that person someone we could reach out to? Out of our abundance, maybe there is room to add some people to our team.

QUESTIONS

WHY IS IT SOMETIMES EASIER TO KEEP TO OURSELVES AND KEEP OUR STRESSES OR INSECURITIES HIDDEN?

WHAT CHANGES IN OUR HEARTS AND MINDS WHEN WE SHARE WITH PEOPLE AND ALLOW THEM TO LIGHTEN OUR LOAD?

WHO IS SOMEONE WHO IS ALREADY YOUR *SUPERADDED*? A PERSON WHO IS ON YOUR TEAM, CONSTANTLY FIGHTING FOR YOU AND LIFTING YOU UP?

WHAT IS A WAY THAT YOU CAN ENGAGE WITH YOUR COMMUNITY MORE THIS WEEK? THINK ON ASKING SOMEONE OUT TO LUNCH. THINK ON SCHEDULING A TRIP WITH A FRIEND. SIMPLE CAN STILL BE SUPER.

PRAYER

God, help me be intentional with my community. Reveal to me the other teammates You'd like on my team, and the ways I can stretch myself to be intentional with others. Thank You for those I already have fighting alongside of me. Thank You for each person who has superadded onto my life. Help me think of ways to connect with them, and engage with them.

Amen.

SUPER EXTRA

++

THINK OF THREE PEOPLE WHO ADD ONTO YOUR LIFE. TEXT OR EMAIL THEM SOME ENCOURAGING WORDS. LET THEM KNOW YOU'RE THINKING OF THEM. SAY A PRAYER FOR THEM AND WHAT THEY MAY BE GOING THROUGH, AND ASK THAT GOD WOULD ADD ONTO THEIR LIVES AS THEY HAVE ADDED ONTO OTHERS. LET THEM KNOW THEY ARE YOUR *SUPERADDED*.

CHAPTER 04: SUPERADDED REST & SUPERADDED BEAUTY

"Beloved, I pray that you may prosper in all things and be in health, just as your soul prospers." 3 John 1:2 (NKJV)

Before we can prosper—before we can be well, before we can have abundant lives—first and foremost, our souls must be well.

Mark 8:36-37 says, **"For what will it profit a man if he gains the whole world, and loses his own soul? Or what will a man give in exchange for his soul?"** (NKJV)

In these verses, Jesus is saying that there is no true success without a healthy soul. We can reach our career goals, make lots of money, and seem very impressive on the outside, but it is pointless if at the end of the day our insides are in ruins. What value is there in the world's approval if, in the process, we traded it for the wellness of our souls?

"Are you tired? Worn out? Burned out on religion? Come to me. Get away with me and you'll recover your life. I'll show you how to take a real rest. Walk with me and work with me—watch how I do it. Learn the unforced rhythms of grace. I won't lay anything heavy or ill-fitting on you. Keep company with me and you'll learn to live freely and

lightly." Matthew 11:28-30 (MSG)

God wants to bring rest to our souls. To the tired, worn out, burned out, stressed out, exhausted, over-worked, under-appreciated, workaholics, and busy bees Jesus says, **"Get away with me and you'll recover your life."**

Jesus wants to fill up our empty souls. He wants to **"recover"** all that's been worn out. He wants to restore all that's been broken.

Many of us—even the most well-intentioned of us—have traded rest for hustling for success—working ourselves to the bone week in and week out no matter the cost. Some of us have traded rest for our obsession with social media—allowing apps that are meant for fun and enjoyment to become unhealthy addictions that consume our time, minds, and emotions. Some of us have traded rest for worry about how we are perceived—caring more about the image and the person others *think* we are rather than the person we actually are and wasting our time living up to standards that are changing every minute.

Whatever we have traded rest for, Jesus wants to lift those burdens, subtract those obsessions, and come into our lives to add on something better, something more. He wants to show us what it's like to walk with Him. He wants to expose us to the beauty of resting, being still, and finding joy in Him. Ultimately, He wants us to **"live freely and lightly."** The abundant life He came to give us involves a light load, a free life, and a rested soul.

A *perissos* life is also filled with beauty.

In Genesis 2:8-9 we learn about the original home God made for humans, the initial habitat for our souls:

"The Eternal God planted a garden in the east in Eden—a

place of utter delight—and placed the man whom He had sculpted there. In this garden, He made the ground pregnant with life—bursting forth with nourishing food and luxuriant beauty. He created trees, and in the center of this garden of delights stood the tree of life and the tree of the knowledge of good and evil." (VOICE)

God first created a playground.

He didn't create a church building. He didn't create an office. He created a beautiful, restful, fun-filled, open-aired garden, blooming with color and life... *a place of utter delight.*

God wants us to relish in His creation. God wants us to find beauty in the seemingly ordinary. God wants us to enjoy the mundane. God wants us to go out of our way to see, hear, and enjoy beauty, to *search* for it, and to experience joy through it.

What fills your soul?

What are ways that you can regularly find rest in God?

What are ways that you can habitually enjoy God's beauty?

I have a group of friends who love hiking; they make it a point to enjoy God's creation together by blazing trails at least once a month.

I have a friend who finds rest in God by waking up 45 minutes early to make coffee while worshipping God through singing, then reading the Bible and praying, all before her kids wake up. She calls it the best 45 minutes of her day.

One way I regularly find rest and beauty is in taking care of my plants. We have a lot of greenery in our house—a superadded amount. My husband calls it my indoor garden. And we also have (too) many plants on our outdoor patio. I love being a plant mama. It is so restful for me to turn on music, a podcast, or sometimes nothing at all, and just water, feed, trim, and take care of my plants. Their beauty fills me and rests my mind. I've also created a little plant corner with one of my favorite, most comfy chairs amongst some of my favorite billowing leaves. In this corner, I love to rest in God through reading about Him, through talking with Him, and, at times, through writing. I wanted to make it a space that I loved, that brought me enjoyment and rest. This little indoor garden corner is simple, but so very serene to me and fills up my soul.

Each one of us fills up differently.

Some of us like to hike, run, read, fish, or garden. Some of us still need to experiment with hobbies and see what truly fills us. Some of us have to find new soul-filling habits and traditions when our environments change. Living in California, my husband and I like to rest and fill up by going to the beach. When we lived in Alaska, we liked to road trip to glaciers and hike snowy trails. It's not a perfect science. It's just honest soul care right where you are.

God wants to super-add onto our souls.

There is no profit, no success, and no abundant life without a healthy soul.

We must make soul-care a priority. We must find moments to rest in His presence. We must find our playgrounds—our moments of beauty. Once we do, our days will be truly *abundant.*

QUESTIONS

WHAT ARE THINGS THAT GET IN THE WAY OF MAKING TIME FOR YOUR SOUL?

WHAT IS A WAY THAT YOU FIND REST IN GOD? HOW CAN YOU MAKE REST A PRIORITY AND HABIT IN YOUR LIFE?

WHAT IS A WAY THAT YOU ENJOY GOD'S BEAUTY? HOW CAN YOU MAKE ENJOYMENT A PRIORITY AND HABIT IN YOUR LIFE?

PRAYER

God, I want to rest in You *more*. I want to enjoy Your creation *more*. I want to find beauty in the seemingly mundane around me. I want to make time where I used to think there was no time. Help me discover the things that fill my soul. Help me be honest with what parts of the day I can spend a little more time with You. I want to enjoy You and the world You created *more*.

Amen.

SUPER EXTRA

LATER IN THIS BOOK WE WILL ALSO TALK ABOUT WORSHIP, HEAVENLY INTERRUPTIONS, AND OTHER THINGS THAT OUR SOULS WERE *MADE* FOR. THERE'S A LOT GOD WANTS FOR OUR SOULS!

THIS WEEK, COMMIT TO **ONE WAY** OF RESTING IN GOD'S PRESENCE, AND **ONE WAY** OF INDULGING IN HIS BEAUTY. BEGIN EXPLORING THE THINGS THAT FILL YOUR SOUL.

I HOPE YOU *ENJOY*.

CHAPTER 05: SUPERADDED DELIGHT

"He rescued me because he delights in me." Psalm 18:19 (NLT)

Sometimes we can feel like a burden to God.

We've heard names like "Unworthy," "Garbage," "Exhausting," more than we've heard the names "Child of God," "Loved Like Crazy," and "Purposefully Made," and naturally, we tend to believe the names we are the most used to hearing.

At times, we can think it's a drag for God to rescue us, annoying for Him to forgive us, and a burden for Him to answer our prayers, keep us safe, and give us good things.

I love that verse in Psalms because it reminds me of what God actually thinks of me.

I hope this reminds you how God—the Creator of the universe *and* the Designer of every one of your details from your fingertips to your eyebrows to your laugh—thinks of you.

He rescues us because He delights in us.

He delights in our delight.

He wants to set us free because He knows what a free life

feels like.

He longs to forgive us and let us know how forgiven we are because He knows what living guilt-free is like.

He yearns to save us again, craves to rescue us again, and begs for us to put our trust in Him again because He knows He can handle everything we are going through, and He *wants* our load to be light. He *wants* our weights to be carried.

It. Brings. Him. *Joy*.

God is asking us to super-add His delight. Allow Him to rescue us. Allow Him to show up for us. Allow Him to give us joy, and wholeness, and deliverance from whatever is holding us back from living our lives to the *fullest*.

The MSG version translates this verse in a way that I can relate to so much, it's scary:

"I stood there saved—surprised to be loved!"

I too am surprised by this love. I too am surprised that He rescues us out of His delight. I too am surprised that He finds joy in my life being abundant. To say it bluntly—I'm straight up shocked that rescuing me brings God any sort of delight. I know how flawed I am… and so does He.

And yet…

I stand here saved.

I stand here still very surprised to be loved.

My hope for myself and each one of us is that we would add on to God's delight, and allow Him to come into our lives, hear our prayers, heal us from our hurts and deliver us from our brokenness. May we cease and desist listening to and answering to any name or identity that has convinced us that we are a burden to God. Instead, may we invite Him in. May we trust in Him. May we super-add.

QUESTIONS

HOW IS THIS IDEA—THAT GOD RESCUES US BECAUSE HE DELIGHTS IN US—DIFFERENT FROM WHAT YOU MAY HAVE PREVIOUSLY HEARD OR FELT ABOUT GOD?

HAVE THERE BEEN TIMES IN YOUR LIFE WHERE YOU DID NOT KNOW THAT YOUR JOY BRINGS GOD JOY? HAVE YOU, AT TIMES, FELT LIKE A BURDEN? WHAT WOULD IT LOOK LIKE TO CONTINUOUSLY LIVE OUT YOUR DAYS KNOWING THAT KEEPING YOU SAFE BRINGS GOD DELIGHT?

WHAT IS ONE THING THAT YOU CAN GIVE TO GOD TO SUPER-ADD ONTO HIS DELIGHT? WHAT IS A HURT YOU CAN ALLOW HIM INTO? A SITUATION YOU CAN SURRENDER TO HIM? A RELATIONSHIP YOU CAN PRAY TO HIM ABOUT?
TELL HIM. LET HIM IN. SUPER-ADD.

PRAYER

God, I want to add on to your delight.
Please, rescue me. Replace this hurt with healing.
Replace this fear with peace. Replace this doubt with safety. Fill me with joy. Help me remember each day that you delight in me, and that you love being there for me.

Amen.

CHAPTER 06: SUPERADDED OPENNESS

"I can't tell you how much I long for you to enter this wide-open, spacious life. We didn't fence you in. The smallness you feel comes from within you. Your lives aren't small, but you're living them in a small way. I'm speaking as plainly as I can and with great affection. Open up your lives. Live openly and expansively!" 2 Corinthians 6:11-13 (MSG)

In this passage, an apostle named Paul is writing to his friends, the church in Corinth. Paul and his companions had opened up to and given much towards this church, and he is asking them to also open up. He sees that they are closed off and is urging them to stop stifling their own growth, affection, and lives, and to instead, **"live openly and expansively!"**

For many of us, we can relate to this church in Corinth.

Parts of us are a bit closed off.

In the first few chapters of this book, we've learned a lot about the life God wants for us. However, some of us might feel like we've already missed out on God's *best*. Perhaps we don't have the team we want. Maybe we don't yet have lives of habitual rest and enjoying God's beauty. Add that with now knowing that God delights in rescuing us, and it's a lot to take in. It's still a surprise to a lot of us.

For some of us, for so long, our lives have felt like one subtraction after another.

And maybe, they have been.

But this is *why* Jesus came.

In John 10:10, this book's main verse, we read not just of Jesus' main purpose, but the Enemy's as well.

"The thief's purpose is to steal and kill and destroy." (NLT)

The Enemy loves to subtract.

His whole *purpose* is to steal our hope, *kill* our confidence, and *destroy* our joy, our self-worth, and our relationships. His entire existence is about taking good thing after good thing away from our lives. His main goal is to leave us, time and time again, *without*.

And for some of us, we can vividly think of the times the Enemy has stolen from us.

Events we've experienced have caused us to close up. Deaths in our lives have caused us to shut down, build walls, and dream small. These hurts have caused us to be too afraid to want, hope, or reach for anything *more*.

We are living our lives in a small way, and yet, **"our lives are not small."**

Enter: Jesus.

The thief comes **"to steal, and to kill, and to destroy. I have come that they may have life, and that they may have it more abundantly."** (NKJV)

Jesus knows that our lives, and our joys have been tampered with.

He came to reclaim what was stolen from us.

Jesus came to bridge the gap between us and God that sin, sadness, and brokenness had created.

He came not just to replace and fill into what was empty, but to fill us *over* the brim, *above* and *beyond*, *exceeding* expectation, and *abundantly*.

No matter what was taken.

No matter what we feel we've missed.

No matter what situations feel hopeless.

Jesus wants us to open up our hearts to Him and to invite Him to super-add onto our lives.

For some of us, this is going to take a lot more courage than others.

For some of us, we'll have to confront what was stolen.

For some of us, we'll have to allow Him into places we've *never* invited Him into before.

For some of us, we never imagined we'd open up to God, to others, or to the person we once hoped we would be again.

2 Corinthians 1:10 says, **"He has delivered us from such a deadly peril, and he will deliver us again. On him we have set our hope that he will continue to deliver us."** (NIV)

Through Jesus, God wants to deliver us again, and again, and again—and abundantly *more* than we've ever imagined.

We want Him to heal *this* hurt? He wants to heal *all* of our hurts.

We want Him to redeem *that* relationship? He wants to redeem *all* of our relationships.

We want Him to help us achieve all our dreams and our goals? He has even bigger, even greater, even crazier and more abundant dreams for us than we could ever have for ourselves.

And—He never grows tired of doing it. Jesus' main purpose was to give us life to the fullest. Whenever we forfeit it, or whenever it's taken from us, He wants to rescue us, and fill us up, again and again.

Let us super-add our openness.

Let us stretch our hearts a little more.

Let us tear down these walls a little more.

Let us *dare* to live openly, and expansively, and just see what He does.

QUESTIONS

WHAT ARE WAYS THE ENEMY HAS STOLEN, KILLED, OR DESTROYED SOMETHING IN YOUR LIFE?

WHAT ARE WAYS THAT YOU FEEL YOUR HEART HAS BEEN CLOSED OFF TO GOD, CLOSED OFF TO OTHER PEOPLE, OR CLOSED OFF TOWARDS WANTING MORE FOR YOURSELF?

WHAT IS YOUR FEAR IN OPENING UP?

WHAT IS YOUR HESITATION IN WANTING MORE?

WHAT ARE THINGS—SINCE YOU CAN ASK GOD TO HEAL, REDEEM, AND RESTORE ANYTHING—YOU WANT TO PRAY ABOUT AND INVITE GOD INTO?

PRAYER

Pray an honest prayer, from your own heart, in your own words, about the things that have closed up the walls in your heart. Invite God in to heal, redeem, and reclaim what the Enemy has stolen.

In the name of Jesus. *Amen.*

SUPER EXTRA

++

I CHALLENGE YOU, THROUGHOUT THE REST OF THIS BOOK, TO APPROACH EACH CHAPTER WITH SUPERADDED OPENNESS, AND ALLOW YOURSELF TO SEE AND EXPERIENCE THE ABUNDANCE, HEALING, AND WHOLENESS GOD WANTS TO ADD ONTO YOUR LIFE.

CHAPTER 07: SUPERADDED PRAYER

SUPER-ADDING BOLDNESS ONTO OUR REQUESTS TO GOD

I can't believe I almost *didn't* ask for more.

In the intro to this book, I shared about the prayer I once prayed, my request for God to *"pour it out, pile it on, and super-add."*

I wanted more—in my outlook on life, in my relationships, in my job, in my marriage, in my routines, in how I loved people, in how I saw people, in how I knew God, and how I spent time with Him. And I didn't want to settle for anything less than what He could possibly have in store for me. I didn't want to be anyone less than the woman I could be. I didn't want to live a life that was haunted by all the could-have-beens. So I asked God—whatever He had—to add it on.

I couldn't have imagined then the **more** that God had for me, that I had not yet asked for, not yet sought out, and not yet pursued.

In Matthew 7:7-8 Jesus says, **"Just ask and it will be given to you; seek after it and you will find. Continue to knock and the door will be opened for you. All who ask receive. Those who seek, find what they seek. And he who knocks, will have the door opened."** (VOICE)

Are we praying big enough prayers?

Are we asking God for the craziest, greatest, most sincere desire of our hearts?

Are we aware of the admission we have to enter into God's presence with bold requests?

Jesus tells us to keep asking, stay seeking, and continue knocking. Don't stop. Don't hesitate. Don't second-guess. Then—be ready to receive, anticipate that you'll find, and be prepared and willing when He opens all kinds of doors.

There is **so much more** that God has in store for us. And He so desires to give it to us. He longs to bless us. He hopes to stretch us so that we can receive even more. He is the Increaser—He loves adding on. And He loves our prayers for His addition.

I like how Hebrews 4:14-16 puts it:

"Now that we know what we have—Jesus, this great High Priest with ready access to God—let's not let it slip through our fingers. We don't have a priest who is out of touch with our reality. He's been through weakness and testing, experienced it all—all but the sin. So let's walk right up to him and get what he is so ready to give. Take the mercy, accept the help." (MSG)

The VOICE translation puts verse 16 this way, **"Let us step boldly to the throne of grace."**

Let us not allow the access we have through Jesus to slip through our fingers.

Let us not pretend like Jesus doesn't understand the desires of our hearts.

Let us walk up to Jesus, approach His throne with boldness, let our desires be known with confidence, and receive **"what he is so ready to give."**

Let us super-add onto our prayers.

Now, about that prayer for *more...*

I so want this for you. I so want you to pray for God to add His abundance onto your life. I so wish I was sitting across from you at a coffee table right now, able to tell you of all the things He has done in my life since praying this prayer, and how it's changed me forever.

But I also want to be honest. It wasn't an easy prayer to pray. And it wasn't an easy prayer to get answered. The seasons that followed that prayer were filled with subtraction—subtracting unhealthy relationships, subtracting unwise habits, subtracting prides that I held tight to, and so much more. There were times I felt like I was losing more than I was gaining, and the truth of some of those circumstances coming into the light hurt deeply.

But then there was room.

There was room for God's addition. There was room for His thoughts to come into my thoughts. There was room for His perspective to become my perspective. There was room for more healthy, uplifting, godly relationships. There was more time for the things that God values. There was more space for things that filled me. There was more peace where there used to be stress. There was more confidence where there used to be doubt.

As I continued to pray for His *more*, His *perissos*, as I eagerly worked on my heart to see what I was holding onto, and as I was continuously and intentionally getting rid of the habits and the attitudes that were keeping me from God's best, there was an *abundance* that was piled onto my life.

This prayer rocks some things in our lives.

And it's a prayer I'm convinced God wants us to pray.

He wants to show up in ways we've never imagined. He wants to subtract the things that have blocked us from His excessive goodness. He wants room to do *above and beyond* what is necessary in our lives. He wants us to break free from lives of settling for less.

I am continuously praying this prayer. I am asking, seeking, and knocking.

I challenge you to do the same.

Let's super-add onto our prayers.

Let's speak boldly and honestly to God about all that's in our hearts.

And let's pray that He would pour out, pile on, and super-add onto our lives.

Then—let's be prepared and willing when He opens all those doors.

QUESTIONS

HOW DO YOU TYPICALLY APPROACH GOD IN PRAYER? WHEN DO YOU SPEAK TO HIM AND WHAT SORT OF THINGS DO YOU SAY TO HIM AND ASK HIM FOR?

WHAT WOULD IT LOOK LIKE TO ADD MORE BOLDNESS AND MORE CONFIDENCE ONTO YOUR PRAYERS?

WHAT ARE SOME DESIRES OF YOUR HEART THAT YOU COME TO GOD WITH RIGHT NOW?

PRAYER

I

I encourage you to pray a bold prayer.
I encourage you to make your requests known to God with confidence. And I encourage you to ask Him for all He has for you—a life abundant, no less. Say words honestly from your heart. Here were mine not too long ago, and these words are still my prayer today:

God, You know I'm ready. I know I'm ready. I'm not playing around. I want more. Give me all that You have for me. Don't hold back. I want a life abundant, no less. Pour it out. Pile it on. Super-add. I don't want to miss one thing. Amen.

MY SUPERADDED LIFE

THIS WEEK I WILL SUPER-ADD:

IN MY COMMUNITY:

With a specific person, relationship, spouse, child, friend, or group of friends...

IN MY RELATIONSHIP WITH GOD:

A habit to enjoy Him more...

IN MY PERSONAL LIFE:

Something that brings you joy, fills up your soul, refreshes your mind, or refocuses your goals...

ONTO SOMEONE ELSE:

A way to super-add onto someone else's life...

I'M EMB

A LIFE O

BRACING

OF MORE

PART  TWO

CHAPTER 08: SUPERADDED EARTH

BRINGING HEAVEN DOWN TO EARTH

In Matthew 6:10, Jesus teaches His disciples how to pray. Within His prayer, Jesus says to God,

"Your kingdom come, your will be done, on earth as it is in heaven." (NIV)

Jesus shows us to pray for something very bold, over the top, and extravagant indeed—for aspects of Heaven to be brought down to manifest *during our lifetime* on this planet.

Here we discover that even on this side of eternity it is possible to experience some of the joys that God has for us in a heavenly realm.

Here we see that God desires His will in Heaven to come down to us—*now*.

Here we discover how we should be praying—and how we should be living.

The Bible tells us that Heaven is a place where we are in a continuous state of worshipping God (Revelation 5:13) and enjoying His presence (Revelation 21:3).

"On Earth as it is in Heaven."

Heaven is a place where we see God personally, know God intimately (1 Corinthians 13:12), and are continuously resting in Him (Revelation 14:13).

"On Earth as it is in Heaven."

Heaven is a place of inclusion, unity, and unending community. Revelation 7:9-10 tells us that the crowd in Heaven was **"too huge to count. Everyone was there—all nations and tribes, all races and languages,"** worshipping God together. (MSG)

"On Earth as it is in Heaven."

Heaven is a place of banquets, feasting, and tables filled with people from all nations, with one Father, one God, in community, eating well together (Matthew 8:11).

"On Earth as it is in Heaven."

What would it look like to live our lives super-adding Heaven onto this Earth? What would it look like to be vessels God uses to carry out His will, His goodness, and His joy on this side of eternity? What would it look like to live lives *practicing* Heaven?

Of course, Earth is a flawed place and there are many things that we will not yet completely experience until this world has passed and Heaven is fully here.

But until it's here in its fullness, it is here in moments.

It's here when we ask God for His will to be done.

It's here when we unashamedly worship Him.

It's here when we rest in His presence.

It's here when we fight for inclusiveness and unity.

It's here when we create and indulge in moments of authentic community.

It's here in the dinner parties.

So the big questions are:

How can we include more people into our circles?

When in our days can we stop and worship Him?

When in our weeks can we set aside time to rest in Him, read about Him, and pray to Him?

How do we fight for those who have turned their backs?

Who is the next person we can invite on a coffee date?

When is the next dinner party that we can plan?

God wants to super-add Heaven onto Earth. He wants His kingdom and His will to carry out here, as it is in Heaven.

In our actions. In our words. In our prayers. In our worship. In our pursuit to see His will done before anyone else's.

Every day of our lives...

May we practice Heaven.

QUESTIONS

WHAT ARE WAYS YOU CAN PRACTICE HEAVEN:

IN WORSHIP?
IN KNOWING AND RESTING IN GOD?
WITH RADICAL INCLUSION?
WITH COMMUNITY CREATING?

HOW CAN YOU COMMIT TO BRINGING HEAVEN DOWN TO EARTH, THIS WEEK, THIS MONTH, AND THIS YEAR?

WHAT WOULD IT LOOK LIKE IF YOUR ENTIRE COMMUNITY WAS COMMITTED TO PRACTICING HEAVEN?

PRAYER

God, may Your Kingdom come, may Your will be done, on Earth as it is in Heaven. May it be done in my attitude, in my actions, and in my time. May it be done in my home, my community, and this world. Help me see the ways that I can bring Heaven into my relationships, my church, and each of my communities. I want to be a part of bringing Heaven down to Earth.

Amen.

CHAPTER 09: SUPERADDED WORSHIP & A SUPERADDED SOUL

"For as long as we are here, we do not live in any permanent city, but are looking for the city that is to come. Through Jesus, then, let us keep offering to God our own sacrifice, the praise of lips that confess His name without ceasing." Hebrews 13:14-15 (VOICE)

As we await our soul's true home, we are able to encounter God, and His sweet, peaceful presence through worship. We touched briefly on this in the last chapter, and now we're super-adding some more thought…

Revelation 21:3 says, **"See, the home of God is with *His* people. He will live among them; They will be His people, And God Himself will be with them."** (VOICE)

God's home is with His people.

His entire goal from the beginning of time has been to live closely amongst us. That's what everything He's ever done in history has been about—taking away anything that stood in the way of that, breaking down every barrier, and bridging every gap through giving His words, His ways, and giving us the ultimate connection between us and Him—Jesus, the One He sent to give us an abundant life.

God's home is with us, and our home is with Him. Though worship is about adoring God alone, it is us—the worshippers—who are filled up by worshipping Him. When we worship Him, we are entering into His magnificent presence and the comfort of our souls being at home with Him.

In Psalm 63:1-5a, King David writes,

"O True God, You are my God, *the One whom I trust.*
I seek You *with every fiber of my being.*
In this dry and weary land with no water in sight,
my soul is dry and longs for You.
My body aches for You, *for Your presence.*
I have seen You in Your sanctuary
and have been awed by Your power and glory.
Your steadfast love is better than life itself,
so my lips will give You *all* my praise.
I will bless You with every breath of my life;
I will lift up my hands in *praise* to Your name.
My soul overflows with satisfaction..." (VOICE)

David is seeking God with *every* fiber.

He aches to experience *all* of God's presence, power, and glory.

His lips are giving God *all* His praises.

He is blessing the Lord with *every* breath.

And in turn... His soul *overflows* with satisfaction.

God wants to super-add onto our souls. He wants to fill us up with peace in our minds, joy in our hearts, and certainty in our spirits. Our souls have access to God's wondrous satisfaction as we continuously—with every fiber in our being—worship Him. His presence will overflow in our lives... above and beyond what we thought possible.

Our souls were meant to face towards God. When they do, our nomadic hearts have returned home.

In the MSG translation, Psalm 63:3 reads: **"In your generous love I am really living at last! My lips brim praises like mountains."**

May our worship towards God pour out over the brim and flood over like fountains. May we—as the writer of Hebrews 13 wrote—praise His name **"without ceasing."** May we adore Him for who He is and all He has done **"without ceasing."** May we sing of His goodness, His grace, and His power **"without ceasing."** May we super-add onto our adoration towards Him and super-add onto the time we allot to do so. Through His generous love we will be **"really living at last!"** Our days will be filled with abundance. Our souls will receive *perissos*.

Psalm 103:1,5 says:

"O my soul, *come*, praise the Eternal with all that is in me—*body, emotions, mind, and will—every part of who I am*—praise His holy name... *When your soul is famished and withering*, He fills you with good *and beautiful* things, satisfying you as long as you live. He makes you *strong* like an eagle, restoring your youth." (VOICE)

God longs to fill our souls with good and beautiful things. May our souls—our body, emotions, mind and will—praise Him, rest in Him, and invite Him in. We will find our life abundant here in these moments—here, at home.

QUESTIONS

WHAT WOULD IT LOOK LIKE TO CONTINUOUSLY SUPER-ADD YOUR WORSHIP TO GOD THIS MONTH?

HOW DOES YOUR SOUL FEEL WHEN YOU WORSHIP HIM?

HOW WOULD YOUR LIFE BE DIFFERENT IF YOU WERE IN A CONSTANT STATE OF FINDING MOMENTS AND METHODS TO WORSHIP HIM MORE, WITHOUT CEASING, AND BRIMMING OVER WITH PRAISES?

PRAYER

Pray your own prayer and speak your own words of worship to God today.

God, I want to worship You more. I want to love on You more. I want to praise You without ceasing. I want my soul to come back home. Help me discover more ways and moments where can I direct my attention towards You, encounter Your presence, and continuously bring Heaven down to Earth, and into my day-to-day life.

Amen.

SUPER EXTRA

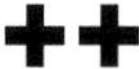

IN THIS MOMENT, PAUSE, AND WORSHIP GOD.

IF YOU'RE ALONE AT HOME,
PLAY A WORSHIP SONG AND SING ALONG.

IF YOU'RE ON THE BUS, LOOK UP A SCRIPTURE VERSE
ON YOUR PHONE AND HONESTLY REFLECT ON IT.

IF YOU'RE ON YOUR LUNCH BREAK AT WORK, SILENTLY
PRAY TO GOD AND SHOWER HIM WITH THANKSGIVING.

AT THE VERY LEAST, WHEREVER YOU ARE, PAUSE,
TURN YOUR SOUL'S ATTENTION TO HIM, AND SPEAK WORDS
OF LOVE, GRATITUDE, AND ADORATION TOWARDS HIM.

CHAPTER 10: SUPERADDED TRUTH

THE WORD OF GOD SHOWS US WHAT TO ADD + SUBTRACT

"The instructions of the Lord are perfect,
reviving the soul.
The decrees of the Lord are trustworthy,
making wise the simple.
The commandments of the Lord are right,
bringing joy to the heart.
The commands of the Lord are clear,
giving insight for living.
Reverence for the Lord is pure,
lasting forever.
The laws of the Lord are true;
each one is fair.
They are more desirable than gold,
even the finest gold.
They are sweeter than honey,
even honey dripping from the comb."
Psalm 19:7-10 (NLT)

The Word of God is filled with marvelously-freeing, life-giving, game-changing truths. These words *revive the soul.*

God wants to super-add truth into our lives.

Filled with wisdom and insight, these truths are **"sweeter**

than honey" and **"more desirable than gold."**

By making the reading of His Word and the listening to His truths a conscious, continuous discipline, our lives go through a *soul revival*, and we add on some wondrous, healing truths that our souls need to know:

The truth about who we are and what our value is.

The truth about how we should approach people.

The truth about God, what He is like, and *all* that He is saying.

The truth about how we get the *most* out of life.

2 Timothy 3:16-17 says:

"All of Scripture is God-breathed; *in its* inspired *voice, we hear* useful teaching, rebuke, correction, *instruction*, and training for a life that is right so that God's people may be up to the task ahead and have all they need to accomplish every good work." (VOICE)

Included in God's truths are instructions of things to subtract. His Word challenges us in areas we are struggling in. It calls us out on our sins, on anything that separates us from God. And it shows us how we are settling for lives that are short of what God has for us.

"Those devoted to instruction will prosper *in goodness*; those who trust in the Eternal will experience His favor." Proverbs 16:20 (VOICE)

The MSG translates Proverbs 16:20 like this: **"It pays to take life seriously; things work out when you trust in God."**

We can sometimes see God's truths and instructions as negative or bothersome or see the Bible as a book filled with restrictions.

And yet, everything God asks of us is meant so that we *prosper.*

God wants to add favor onto our lives. He wants to pour out and pile on all of His goodness. Everything He asks us to subtract is a means to all of this addition. He wants us to be rid of anything that stands in the way of that crazy abundance, that overflowing favor, and His excessive goodness. He doesn't want to give the Enemy *any* power to *steal, kill,* or *destroy* anything in our lives.

When we are devoted to His truths, His words, and His ways, when we take this life He gave us seriously, we will experience this life *abundantly.*

2 Corinthians 6:1 says, **"Please don't squander one bit of this marvelous life God has given us."** (MSG)

Let us take hold of this marvelous life.

Let us go out of our way, take command of our schedules, and find even *more* time to immerse ourselves in the truths found in the Word of God.

Let us heartily receive the rebuke, the corrections, and God's loving, instructed subtractions, and let us eagerly seize the wisdom, the beauty, the joy, and God's miraculous, life-giving additions. **All** of His truths are a means for us to prosper.

Let's live out these truths every day.

Let's super-add onto our souls.

Let's begin a *soul revival.*

QUESTIONS

WHY DO YOU THINK IT'S SOMETIMES EASIER TO THINK OF GOD'S INSTRUCTIONS AS SUBTRACTIONS, INSTEAD OF THE MEANS TO ADDITIONS?

WHAT ARE THINGS YOU LEARN AND FEEL WHEN YOU READ THE WORD OF GOD?

WHAT ARE WAYS YOU CAN COMMIT TO REVIVING YOUR SOUL? WHAT IS A DISCIPLINE YOU CAN BEGIN IN ORDER TO READ THE TRUTHS IN THE WORD OF GOD MORE?

PRAYER

I

God, I want a soul revival.
I want Your truths so deeply rooted and alive within me that I am in a constant state of walking in and living by Your truths. I want to super-add all the wisdom and joy and instructions You have for me. I want to subtract all that stands in the way. Show me the ways I can indulge in Your truths and in Your Word more.

Amen.

SUPER EXTRA

++

HONESTLY ASSESS WHAT IS THE BEST TIME OF DAY AND THE BEST MEDIUM FOR YOU TO EXPERIENCE THE WORD OF GOD. PERHAPS YOU'VE TRIED TO DO IT AT NIGHT, BUT YOU'RE REALLY A MORNING PERSON. MAYBE YOU'VE TRIED TO READ THE BIBLE FOR LONG PERIODS OF TIME, BUT YOU'VE GOTTEN DISTRACTED. THINK ON YOUR SPECIFIC SCHEDULE AND PREFERENCES. CONSIDER WAKING UP A LITTLE EARLIER OR DOWNLOADING THE BIBLE ON AUDIOBOOK SO YOU CAN LISTEN ON YOUR COMMUTE. TAKE A MINUTE TO SERIOUSLY REFLECT ON HOW YOU CAN HABITUALLY SOAK IN GOD'S TRUTHS MORE.

MAKE A COMMITMENT.
TELL SOMEONE SO THEY HELP KEEP YOU TO IT.
SUPER-ADD TRUTH INTO YOUR DAILY AND WEEKLY ROUTINES.

CHAPTER 11: SUPERADDED REVERSAL

UPSIDE-DOWN LIVING. HEAVEN-TO-EARTH-BRINGING. OPPOSITE DAY EVERY DAY.

In the book of Matthew, Jesus flips the kingdom of the world upside down.

"'You have been taught to love your neighbor and hate your enemy. But I tell you this: love your enemies. Pray for those who torment you and persecute you... You are called to something higher: Be perfect, as your Father in heaven is perfect.'" Matthew 5:43, 44, 48 (VOICE)

"...the disciples came to Jesus and questioned Him about the kingdom of heaven. [A disciple asked,] 'In the kingdom of heaven, who is the greatest?' Jesus called over a little child. He put His hand on the top of the child's head. [Jesus replied,] 'This is the truth: unless you change and become like little children, you will never enter the kingdom of heaven. In that kingdom, the most humble who are most like this child are the greatest.'" Matthew 18:1-4 (VOICE)

"Here it is again, the Great Reversal: many of the first ending up last, and the last first." Matthew 20:16 (MSG)

Living a superadded life, super-adding the mindset of

Heaven, and super-adding the perspective of Jesus requires a superadded reversal.

The Kingdom of the Earth says:

"Put your enemies in their place."
"Tear their reputations down!"
"Be the greatest."
"Be a king."
"Let people know you're ahead!"
"Be first."

The Kingdom of Heaven says:

"Pray for your enemies."
"Shower them with love and words of kindness."
"Humility is the greatest."
"Have faith like a child."
"Let people know their potential, their value, and their worth, more than you tell them about yours."
"Don't obsess about being first—many of the first will be last. Don't waste your life away, consumed with being number one, that's not a worthwhile goal."

These two kingdoms are not just a little different from one another—they are super opposite.

We can't live for both.

For many of us, there are situations in our lives that we need to flip completely upside-down.

For some of us, there are emotions and attitudes that need to undergo this Great Reversal.

There are some habits that we can practice in order for this

Heavenly mindset to become our own.

For me, when it comes to people who have torn me down, never apologized to me, or have been difficult to love, there are two things I have learned to do in order to "reverse" in my own life.

1 – I pray for them.

2 – When good things happen in their lives, I say, "Good for them."

Sounds simple, right? But I have to be honest, it wasn't always simple for me. For a while, I faked it until I made it. I would whisper those prayers and quietly say this phrase under my breath, and those words would barely make it off my tongue. But as I continuously placed my feelings upside-down, as I mentally put myself in the back of the line, as I constantly prayed that these other people would be healed, and whole, and that God would have His will in their lives, and as I continuously practiced saying to myself and to God behind closed doors, "Good for them," it slowly became natural. I started believing what I was saying. I began seeing people through a truly different perspective. Over time, when I would see those people succeed, I would smile, and be genuinely glad for them. There were times when their names would come up in conversation and I would speak highly of them to others. Not because it was fair—grace isn't fair—but because I had made a decision to answer to the call of, as Matthew 5:48 puts it, **"something higher."** I had made the decision to have a life of *more*.

I had realized that by being consumed by my negative thoughts and wounded emotions, the Enemy was stealing, killing, and destroying my joy, my time, and the abundant life that Jesus came to give me.

Heaven's Great Reversal set me free.

By speaking well of those who were not speaking well of me and by forgiving those who had never said sorry, I was set free. My emotions were set free, my mindset was set free, and the space that those hurts once occupied was now open, available, and freed up for something higher, something better, something *more*.

I don't know what this looks like for you. I don't know what situations are filling up your mind's space. Perhaps my go-to "good for them" phrase has really nothing to do with the reversal that's tugging on your heart. There may be a completely different practice or phrase that's coming to your mind.

My hope and prayer is that we would each honestly assess the attitudes and emotions in our lives that need to be flipped around. The ungodly competition, the resentment, the anger—we know what's in our hearts. Once we accept what is there, we can continue to subtract *whatever* is standing in the way of *perissos*—the abundance of good things God has for us, Heaven on Earth kind-of-living, and freed lives that are open and available for a great addition.

QUESTIONS

WHAT IS A SITUATION IN YOUR LIFE THAT YOU KNOW YOU ARE SEEING THROUGH A KINGDOM OF THE WORLD LENS?

WHAT WOULD IT LOOK LIKE TO NOT NEED TO BE FIRST, RIGHT, OR WORSHIPPED IN THIS SITUATION, BUT TO, INSTEAD, FLIP YOUR MINDSET AROUND?

WHAT IS A PRACTICE YOU CAN BEGIN IN YOUR LIFE TO START WALKING IN THIS GREAT REVERSAL?

PRAYER

I

God, help me to not need to be first. Help me to not need to be recognized. Help me to not obsess over getting revenge in every situation I've been hurt in. Help to me live out this Great Reversal. Please show me how. In the moments when I'm consumed with ungodly, prideful emotions, remind me of the decision I've made to answer to "something higher" and to live a life of *more*. I choose Your Kingdom.

Amen.

CHAPTER 12: SUPERADDED CHILDHOODS

"It is your faith in the Anointed Jesus that makes all of you children of God." Galatians 3:26 (VOICE)

Time and time again, the Bible refers to those who receive Jesus and put their faith in Him as *children* of God. In the last chapter we read that Jesus said, **"Unless you change and become like little children, you will never enter the kingdom of heaven."** Matthew 18:3 (VOICE)

Our lives with Jesus—our abundant lives—are meant to be lived as God's **children.**

Being a child is a part of bringing Heaven down to Earth.

This begs the question—what does it mean to live as God's *child*?

We have each had different childhoods. Perhaps some of us had to grow up a little fast, mature a little early, and "being a child" has never really occurred to us. Perhaps some of us don't have fond memories of what our childhood entailed. For some of us, being a child is the opposite of the hard-working, self-sufficient, grown-up lifestyle we've worked hard to attain.

God wants to super-add a childlike faith into our lives and help us **reclaim our childhoods.**

He wants our faith in Him, our trust in Him, and our view of Him to begin again.

John 1:12 says, **"For all who did receive and trust in [Jesus], He gave them the right to be *reborn* as children of God."** (VOICE)

Maybe we haven't been filled with a childlike faith before. Maybe we haven't trusted God or enjoyed God as the ultimate Father—one far better than any of our earthly fathers—before. Or maybe we need to be reminded that when we received Jesus, we had the right to be reborn as God's children. Maybe some of us need to reclaim this truth in our lives and let our perspectives begin again.

Scripture after scripture describes what trusting God and having childlike faith in God is like.

Through the Word of God we discover there is so much more freedom than we have ever imagined.

Through His truths we realize a childhood we can begin, a childhood we can relearn, and a childhood we can reclaim.

What does it mean to live as God's *child*?

To lounge around in grassy fields and just enjoy the sunshine?

Yes.

"God, my shepherd!
I don't need a thing.
You have bedded me down in lush meadows,

you find me quiet pools to drink from.
True to your word,
you let me catch my breath
and send me in the right direction." Psalm 23:1-3 (MSG)

What does it mean to live as God's child?

To be free of the weights of responsibility? To be reckless? To be risky? To be curious? And yet somehow be safe?

Yes.

"Come to Me, all who are weary and burdened, and I will give you rest." Matthew 11:28 (VOICE)

"The minute I said, 'I'm slipping, I'm falling,'
your love, God, took hold and held me fast.
When I was upset and beside myself,
you calmed me down and cheered me up." Psalm 94:18-19 (MSG)

What does it mean to live as God's child?

To play with your friends all the time?

Yes.

We know this! We read this earlier!

"How good and pleasant it is when God's people live together in unity!" Psalm 133:1 (NIV)

What does it mean to live as God's child?

To just be joyful and have fun every day?

Yes.

"Always be full of joy in the Lord. I say it again—rejoice!" Philippians 4:4 (NLT)

What does it mean to live as God's child?

To not be constantly anxious about the future and always worrying about the burdens of the world? To be carefree and trusting?

Yes.

"Give your entire attention to what God is doing right now, and don't get worked up about what may or may not happen tomorrow. God will help you deal with whatever hard things come up when the time comes." Matthew 6:34 (MSG)

"Live carefree before God; he is most careful with you." 1 Peter 5:7 (MSG)

Just like in previous chapters, we read again of playgrounds, rest, and enjoyment.

God is saying to each of us, "Come, be a child. Celebrate all the time. Trust that I am watching you, will carry you, and always want good things for you. Find safety in me. Don't wear the burden of being in charge. Enjoy the world I created for you. Enjoy life with me. Enjoy life with my other children. Have fun. Take risks. Trust me."

My whole life changed the moment I understood that I was always supposed to approach God as a child.

I had to relearn some things.

But I have made the choice to reclaim and—in some ways—begin a childhood.

I have allowed God to subtract my paralyzing fears, worries, and stresses.

I have invited God to super-add a childlike faith and childlike joy into my life.

If you have received Jesus and put your trust in Him, you too have the right to be reborn, to relearn, and to reclaim a childhood.

QUESTIONS

WHAT WAS YOUR CHILDHOOD LIKE? WHAT WERE SOME WAYS YOUR CHILDHOOD WAS IMPERFECT OR TAKEN FROM YOU OR SITUATIONS IN IT THAT MADE YOU GROW UP TOO FAST?

HOW WOULD YOUR LIFE LOOK DIFFERENT IF YOU LIVED IT THROUGH THE LENS OF GOD'S CHILD—ENJOYING GOD AND ENJOYING HIS PEOPLE?

FOR YOU, WHAT HABITS, PERSPECTIVES, OR DECISIONS WOULD YOU NEED TO CHANGE IN ORDER TO LIVE MORE LIKE A CHILD—DELIGHTING IN, TRUSTING IN, AND RESTING IN GOD?

PRAYER

I

God, help me to learn what it means to be Your child. Help me see the situations where I need to trust You more. Help me to be aware of the things I've overlooked that I could be enjoying more. Help me see what I need to relearn. I want to embrace a childlike faith. Help me discover the ways I can reclaim my childhood.

Amen.

SUPER EXTRA

++

WHAT IS SOMETHING FUN YOU WOULD LIKE TO DO THIS WEEK TO ENJOY GOD, ENJOY HIS PEOPLE, OR ENJOY THE WORLD AROUND YOU?

THINK OF A PARK YOU COULD VISIT, SOMEONE TO TAKE TO BREAKFAST, A DATE YOU COULD SURPRISE YOUR SPOUSE WITH, AN ADVENTURE YOU COULD HAVE WITH YOUR DAUGHTER OR SON, A NIGHT OUT YOU COULD PLAN WITH YOUR FRIENDS, A COFFEE SHOP YOU HAVE BEEN WANTING TO TRY OR READ A BOOK IN, A TRIP TO THE BEACH, OR A HIKE IN THE MOUNTAINS. BE CREATIVE. OR BE SIMPLE.

WHAT IS SOMETHING THAT WOULD FILL UP YOUR SOUL AND GIVE YOU CHILDLIKE JOY? THINK OF THAT THING. COMMIT TO DOING IT THIS WEEK.
CALL THAT PERSON, MAKE THAT PLAN, AND ENJOY.

CHAPTER 13: SUPERADDED PEACE

"Celebrate God all day, every day. I mean, *revel* in him! Make it as clear as you can to all you meet that you're on their side, working with them and not against them. Help them see that the Master is about to arrive. He could show up any minute!" Philippians 4:4-5 (MSG)

Continued in verses 6 and 7:

"Don't be anxious about things; instead, pray. Pray about everything. He longs to hear your requests, so talk to God about your needs and be thankful for what has come. And know that the peace of God (a peace that is beyond any and all of our human understanding) will stand watch over your hearts and minds in Jesus, the Anointed One." (VOICE)

I am so desperate for this peace in my life—a peace that is *beyond* any of our human understanding, a peace that *exceeds* our own expectations of peace, a peace that only flows from the outpouring of God. I want an abundance of *that.*

This verse simply outlines how we can have that peace filling up our lives.

1 – Celebrate God, all day every day.
When we wake up, while we go about our days, and as we

go to sleep, let us keep God's goodness at the forefront of our minds and have a posture of worshipping Him. With our words and with our actions let us celebrate Him, honor Him, and point towards Him.

2 – Be gentle, kind, and on other people's side.
I love the phrase in this verse, **"working with them and not against them."** It gives us such a clear picture of what this gentleness looks like practically. It looks like linking up with people. It looks like listening to people. It looks like having empathy for other people's perspectives and hurts. It looks like other people feeling like you are on their team. This is how we show them how present and close the Lord is to us—not by being *against* them, but being *for* them.

3 – Pray instead of worry.
This verse doesn't just leave us at **"don't be anxious."** On its own that phrase would be unhelpful and even condescending because we don't always feel we have control over our anxiety. Instead, it gives us something else to do: pray about all of it. This has been a life-long lesson for me. I can easily get overwhelmed with worry, and, at times, I dwell on all the worse-case scenarios. I constantly need to remind myself to subtract worry and anxiety by instead adding a pattern of prayer—praying for the little things, the big things, the me-things, the them-things, praying repeatedly and nonstop.

4 – Be thankful.
As we speak to God about our needs and desires, let us also vocalize our gratitude for what we do have and what He has done. Not only does this praise and honor Him, but it also reminds us of the situations we've already seen Him in. When we are aware, content, and grateful for what we already have, we become less focused on and less anxious about what we don't.

When we celebrate God daily, are gentle towards others, exchange our worry time for prayer time, and live and speak from a perspective of thankfulness, God's peace will pour out into our lives and overflow to those around us. A superadded peace, a peace above and beyond what we've thought was possible, a peace that is even better and beyond anything we can understand.

QUESTIONS

WHICH OF THESE FOUR THINGS DO YOU WANT TO BE BETTER AT IN YOUR DAY-TO- DAY LIFE?

WHAT IS A WAY THAT YOU CAN PRACTICALLY AND HABITUALLY DO SO?

PRAYER

Pray a prayer to God that—

- Celebrates Him
- Asks to learn how to be more gentle
- Asks for the desire of your heart and speaks of your worries
- Is filled with thankfulness

Pray this prayer from your own heart.
In the name of Jesus. *Amen.*

CHAPTER 14: SUPERADDED INTERRUPTIONS

SUPER-ADDING HIS PRESENCE ONTO OUR DAILY LIVES

One of my favorite ways I super-add onto my life's routines is what I've called a Superadded Walk. Once a week, in the middle of a work day, I leave my office for 20 minutes and take a walk. I have a playlist on my phone filled with some of my favorite worship songs. For the record, I call it my Superadded Walk because that's what I initially titled the playlist I made on my phone and I've never changed it, so boom—it is what it is. No one has time for changing titles. So many buttons and updates—clearly that is *not* the abundant life Jesus came to give us! (P.S.: someone super-add onto my life and help me with technology, please.)

I put on my headphones, cue up the-title-that-shall-not-be-changed-playlist, and stroll around the neighborhood, listening to these soul-filling words, singing the heavenly lyrics within my heart, and praying quietly to God—thanking Him, loving on Him, praying over my circumstances, and the people in my life.

I love changing up my scenery in the middle of my day—seeing bright, budding flowers growing amongst the houses I walk by, neighbors riding their bikes, the energy of the cars gliding along the street. It fills my soul and allows my eyes to enjoy an aesthetic beyond the black, typed letters along my computer screen and my ears to indulge in sounds beyond the Skype "incoming call" jingle. But more than all that, I love interrupting my day to turn my soul's attention God, to focus only on His words and presence, and to invite Him to fill me.

As a creative, these walks have been an added joy. As a child of God, these walks have become essential. I've learned to make time where it doesn't make sense. I've learned that enjoying God is one of the best parts of being alive.

More than ever, I am convinced that the superadded life Jesus came to give us is a life filled with heavenly interruptions—making room, making time, and making exceptions within our schedules to encounter the presence of God.

In Psalm 84:10, King David writes these lyrics:

"Just one day in the courts of Your temple is greater than a thousand anywhere else. I would rather serve as a porter at my God's doorstep than live in luxury in the house of the wicked." (VOICE)

We must find ways to interrupt our daily, weekly, and monthly routines to focus on and get filled up by the Lord.

This will be different for everyone.

For me, once a week (I hope to get this to multiple times a week) I take a walk with my curated playlist. Maybe you clean your house every Tuesday. You could blast some praise and worship music and worship and pray to Him during that time. Or maybe you have an hour commute to work and instead of listening to the radio, you could invest time into finding podcasts and sermons to play that challenge and encourage your heart. You could even do this during your lunch break! In the middle of your workday, while walking the dogs after dinner, or taking your kids to the park—bring your Bible, have your playlists ready, whatever that looks like for you.

Not all of our days, locations, personalities, or interests are the same. But our souls all need these interruptions. One day in His presence is far greater than a thousand somewhere else. Twenty minutes walking with Him on a busy Thursday is far better than 20 years walking alongside anything or anyone else. The more interruptions we can find the better. The more we allow His presence to invade our daily routines the better. This benefits our *lives*, our *souls*, our *perspectives*, and our *attitudes*. So let's not settle for anything less than these super special moments sprinkled into our routines. Let's be honest in assessing what those could be in our own lives, and then be intentional with committing to them and carrying them out.

That's all I have for now. It's time for my walk.

QUESTIONS

WHAT IS A WAY YOU COULD INTERRUPT A DAILY OR WEEKLY ROUTINE TO ENCOUNTER THE PRESENCE OF GOD?

WHAT STEPS WOULD YOU NEED TO TAKE TO KEEP THAT COMMITMENT?

HOW DO YOU THINK YOUR LIFE AND YOUR SOUL WOULD BE DIFFERENT IF IT WAS FILLED WITH HEAVENLY INTERRUPTIONS?

PRAYER

God, show me the ways I can interrupt my routines to make room to encounter You more. I want more heavenly interruptions in my life. I want super-added habits and routines that are designed to focus on and enjoy You. Help me think of ways to add Your presence into my day-to-day life.

Amen.

MY SUPERADDED LIFE

THIS WEEK I WILL SUPER-ADD:

IN MY COMMUNITY:

With a specific person, relationship, spouse, child, friend, or group of friends…

IN MY RELATIONSHIP WITH GOD:

A habit to enjoy Him more…

IN MY PERSONAL LIFE:

Something that brings you joy, fills up your soul, refreshes your mind, or refocuses your goals…

ONTO SOMEONE ELSE:

A way to super-add onto someone else's life…

“PLEASE

DON’T
SQUANDER

OF

2 CORINTHIANS 6:1 (MSG)

ONE BIT

THIS
MARVELOUS

LIFE."

2 CORINTHIANS 6:1 (MSG)

PART 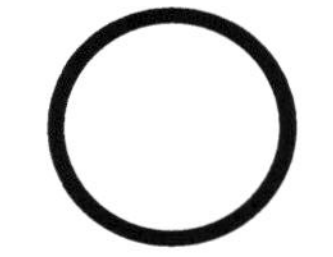 THREE

CHAPTER 15: SUPERADDED PERSPECTIVE

"So if you're serious about living this new resurrection life with Christ, act like it. Pursue the things over which Christ presides. Don't shuffle along, eyes to the ground, absorbed with the things right in front of you. Look up, and be alert to what is going on around Christ—that's where the action is. See things from *his* perspective." Colossians 3:1-2 (MSG)

Have you ever looked down from an elevated point of view? Driven to the top of a hill, hiked to the top of a mountain, or walked to a high point in a park or forest? When we are in traffic or marching through the dirt on our paths, we can only see what's right in front of us and the conditions that immediately surround us.

But then we get to the top. We see all the streets and traveling cars. We see neighborhoods in their grids and the city's energy moving together. We see the trails we walked, the boulders we climbed, and the wind blowing through the trees we ventured around. And all of a sudden, with this different perspective, the view of the same place we were just in is completely different. We don't see the guy that was cutting us off on the road or the rocks that got into our shoes. We take a deep breath and soak in the scenery, the reality of the full picture, from this elevated view.

From this view, some things look smaller. From this view, some things look bigger.

The writer in Colossians is talking about seeing *our lives* from an elevated view.

It can be easy for us to keep our **"eyes to the ground."** It can be natural for us to be **"absorbed with the things right in front of [us]."** It can be difficult when someone says hateful things to us, when someone gets a promotion we didn't, or when we're stressed out about the next step in our lives. It's easy to remain narrow-focused, consumed with the conditions that are only at our parallel-eye view.

This verse reminds us—

One: "Look up."

Look up from this situation that is consuming your mind with negativity.

Look up from the state of your heart that is filled with hatred, competition, and worry.

Look up from the ground you are staring at, the view you are seeing from your own state of pride, selfishness, and fear.

Look up and see what Jesus is doing.

Look up and remind yourself of the things that He cares about, of what He has called **you** to do.

Look up and remind yourself of the person you are when you

are more like Him.

Look up and see Him, pray to Him, think on Him, and let your mind be consumed with His words and His thoughts.

Psalm 121:1-2 says:

"I lift up my eyes to the mountains—
where does my help come from?
My help comes from the Lord,
the Maker of heaven and earth." (NIV)

As we are on our journey here on the ground, let us remember to lift our eyes to the mountains, to what is ahead, to the ultimate goal, and look up towards Heaven—where our ultimate help comes from.

Two: Look down, and "see things from his perspective."

Imagine your circumstance from His point of view. Imagine these streets and these trails from the view on *top* of the mountain. Imagine these relationships, these fears, and these hurts through the lens of Christ.

From this view, some things will look smaller. From this view, some things will look bigger. One thing is for certain, this view is completely different from our own.

Philippians 2:5-8 says:

"...Adopt the mind-set of Jesus the Anointed. *Live with His attitude in your hearts.* Remember:
Though He was in the form of God,
He chose not to cling to equality with God;
But He poured Himself out to *fill a vessel brand new;*
a servant in form

and a man indeed.
The very likeness of humanity,
He humbled Himself,
obedient to death—
a merciless death on the cross!" (VOICE)

The lens of Jesus is a lens of humility, a lens of not holding onto a selfish agenda, a lens of forfeiting pride, rights, and entitlement, a lens of confidence in God, of hope, of love, a lens of forgiveness, and a lens of putting other people first.

The people who spoke hateful words to us need prayer. The people who received the promotions we didn't? Their success doesn't take away from what God is calling *us* to do. The people we feel competitive with? God also has a plan for them and wants to work in their lives.

But how would we see that if we're only looking at our lives from our own point of view?

For many of us, we have a good, well-intentioned outlook on life. We just need to super-add some height to that perspective.

Let us look up. Let us see what Christ is doing, how He is loving, how He is moving, and what He values.

Let us then look down and see the world, our lives, and the lives of the people around us through His elevated point of view.

QUESTIONS

WHY IS IT SOMETIMES HARD TO SEE THINGS THROUGH CHRIST'S PERSPECTIVE?

WHAT IS A SITUATION IN YOUR LIFE THAT YOU WANT TO BEGIN TO SEE FROM AN ELEVATED POINT OF VIEW?

WHEN YOU LOOK UP AT CHRIST, HOW DOES THIS HELP YOUR PERSPECTIVE?

WHEN YOU LOOK DOWN AT YOUR SITUATION FROM HIS POINT OF VIEW, HOW DOES THIS CHANGE HOW YOU SEE IT AND HOW YOU WANT TO APPROACH IT?

WHAT WOULD IT LOOK LIKE TO LIVE WITH THIS SUPERADDED PERSPECTIVE?

PRAYER

God, I want to add some height to my perspective. I'm tired of looking at the ground, absorbed with what's right in front of me. Remind me to look up to You in times of hardship and in times of plenty. Remind me to look down at these same times from Your perspective. I want to live a life seeing things from Your point of view.

Amen.

CHAPTER 16: SUPERADDED CONTENTMENT

This is a superadded passage with superadded truths that we need in our lives—

"I've learned by now to be quite content whatever my circumstances. I'm just as happy with little as with much, with much as with little. I've found the recipe for being happy whether full or hungry, hands full or hands empty. Whatever I have, wherever I am, I can make it through anything in the One who makes me who I am. I don't mean that your help didn't mean a lot to me—it did. It was a beautiful thing that you came alongside me in my troubles.

You Philippians well know, and you can be sure I'll never forget it, that when I first left Macedonia province, venturing out with the Message, not one church helped out in the give-and-take of this work except you. You were the only one. Even while I was in Thessalonica, you helped out—and not only once, but twice. Not that I'm looking for handouts, but I do want you to experience the blessing that issues from generosity.

And now I have it all—and keep getting more! The gifts you sent with Epaphroditus were more than enough, like a sweet-smelling sacrifice roasting on the altar, filling the air with fragrance, pleasing God no end. You can be sure that God will take care of everything you need, his generosity exceeding even yours in the glory that pours from Jesus."
Philippians 4:12-20 (MSG)

This passage begins and ends with an overflowing amount of *contentment.*

The writer, Paul? He's in prison. Not ideal. And he still has joy? I love that. I need that. I want to access that abundance.

Paul has found joy with a little and joy with a lot because Jesus is ultimately who satisfies him, and in Jesus—all Jesus is and all He has done and all He says about him—Paul is content. It's enough for him.

Still, he is so very grateful for the generosity the church in Philippi has shown him. ***"It was a beautiful thing."*** They were superadded givers—when no one else gave, ***"they gave not only once, but twice,"*** and gave ***"more than enough!"***

Paul says, because of their abundance of giving, God will super-add onto their lives as well.

Their giving pleased God to *no end.* God was honored by it. Worshipped by it. Joyful because of it—they brought *God* joy! That's awesome! And in response to their gift—**God will exceed it.**

God will add onto them even more than they were able to add.

This verse doesn't say He will give them whatever they want. It says He will *take care of everything they need.*

That. Is. So. Good.

This is *beyond* money. This is *beyond* nice things. This is a life overflowing with joy and contentment. This is a life of being satisfied with something, Someone, who is beyond material things. This is a life that is not obsessed with money or the need for more possessions, but instead finds freedom in *having enough*, and joy in blessing the Lord through giving.

Superadded contentment is found when we practice superadded generosity.

When we become *givers*, we don't live in the urgency to acquire more than we need. Instead, we become aware of the value of what we already have.

Paul mentions *the blessing that issues from generosity*. In the VOICE translation Paul says, **"I am just looking toward your reward that comes from your gift."** He knows what's coming! He's excited for them. He wants them to experience this same kind of surreal satisfaction.

Just like Paul, we too can be blessed with contentment—joy with a lot and joy with a little, joy all the time and joy no matter what. Fulfillment through Jesus alone. But that doesn't just happen *to* us. It's a blessing as a result of an action: selflessness through giving.

QUESTIONS

WHAT MAKES CONTENTMENT DIFFICULT?

WHAT MAKES GIVING DIFFICULT?

HOW WOULD THE WORLD LOOK DIFFERENT IF EVERYONE HAD SUPERADDED CONTENTMENT?

WHAT IS A WAY YOU CAN GIVE THIS WEEK—ABOVE AND BEYOND WHAT YOU WERE PLANNING TO GIVE?

PRAYER

I

God, I want to live a content life.
I don't want to obsess over things I don't need.
I don't want to stress over what I don't have.
Give me ideas of ways I can give more. Help me
find satisfaction and joy in all I already have.

Amen.

SUPER EXTRA

++

THINK ON A SHELTER OR CLOTHING DRIVE THAT YOU COULD DONATE A BAG OF CLOTHES TO. THINK ON GIVING ABOVE AND BEYOND YOUR NORMAL TITHE AT CHURCH THIS WEEK.

THINK ON A MISSIONARY, MINISTRY, OR CHILD YOU COULD FINANCIALLY SUPPORT. THINK ON SOMEONE WHO COMES UP IN YOUR FACEBOOK FEED THAT IS RAISING MONEY FOR A TRIP THAT YOU COULD DONATE TO.

THINK ON THINGS AROUND YOUR HOME THAT YOU COULD SELL IN ORDER TO HAVE MORE RESOURCES TO GIVE.

GIVING LOOKS DIFFERENT FOR EVERYONE.
TAKE AN HONEST LOOK AT HOW YOU CAN PRACTICE SUPERADDED GENEROSITY THIS WEEK.

CHAPTER 17: SUPERADDED WITH THE EXTRAORDINARY

CRAZY COMPASSION + UNDESERVED LOVE

"If you're listening, here's My message: Keep loving your enemies no matter what they do. Keep doing good to those who hate you. Keep speaking blessings on those who curse you. Keep praying for those who mistreat you. If someone strikes you on one cheek, offer the other cheek too. If someone steals your coat, offer him your shirt too. If someone begs from you, give to him. If someone robs you of your valuables, don't demand them back. Think of the kindness you wish others would show you; do the same for them.

Listen, what's the big deal if you love people who already love you? Even scoundrels do that much! So what if you do good to those who do good to you? Even scoundrels do that much! So what if you lend to people who are likely to repay you? Even scoundrels lend to scoundrels if they think they'll be fully repaid. If you want to be extraordinary—love your enemies! Do good without restraint! Lend with abandon! Don't expect anything in return! Then you'll receive the truly great reward—you will be children of the Most High—for God is kind to the ungrateful and

those who are wicked. So imitate God and be truly compassionate, the way your Father is." Luke 6:27-36 (VOICE)

When I think of being extraordinary, I think of many things: climbing the highest mountains, swimming through billowing rapids, and taking on adventures few have dared to!

This verse talks about something much harder than any of those things.

Love your enemies.

Is it okay for me to say that a big part of me hates that? I'm not a big fan of Jesus asking us to love people who don't love us, to give to people who take from us, and to not even ask for a little something in return. It feels unnatural. And it certainly doesn't seem fair.

It's not natural. And it's not fair.

It's *extraordinary.*

To be kind to those who are ungrateful for our time and our love…

To show compassion to those who take more than they give...

To pray for those who have hurt us…

Love and compassion above and beyond what is necessary, warranted, and deserved?

Jesus wants us to be filled with this kind of *extraordinary.*

It is ordinary to only give to those who give to us. It is typical to only love those who love us. It is assumed that we will play nice with those who play nice with us. And yet Jesus doesn't want us to have an ordinary life. Jesus did not give us an ordinary example to learn from.

"…while we were wasting our lives in sin, God revealed His powerful love to us *in a tangible display*—the Anointed One died for us." Romans 5:8 (VOICE)

At one point this was us. We were not living lives giving towards God.

At some points, it's still us. Wasting our lives in selfishness, pride, and sin.

And yet, God was extraordinary. Even when we didn't deserve any amount of love or compassion. Jesus, God's Son—the greatest gift, the craziest sacrifice, the biggest loss for a Father—died for us. It wasn't natural. It wasn't fair. And it certainly wasn't ordinary.

Jesus calls on us to live our lives filled with this extra, more than enough, above and beyond love and compassion for those who don't even deserve it. The MSG version says Luke 6:35-36 like this: **"You'll never—I promise—regret it. Live out this God-created identity the way our Father lives toward us, generously and graciously, even when we're at our worst. Our Father is kind; you be kind."**

He promises we will not regret living this kind of life.
He speaks of our great reward.
He tells us we will be living as children of the Most High God.

He invites us to a life of imitating and being filled with the extraordinary.

QUESTIONS

WHO IS SOMEONE WHO HAS HURT YOU THAT YOU CAN PRAY FOR RIGHT NOW?

HOW WOULD EMBRACING THIS EXTRAORDINARY CHANGE YOUR PERSPECTIVE OF THE PEOPLE IN YOUR LIFE TODAY?

WHAT WOULD IT LOOK LIKE TO LIVE SUPERADDED WITH THIS EXTRAORDINARY LOVE AND COMPASSION?

PRAYER

I

God, show me how to be this kind of *extraordinary.* May I be so filled with this love and compassion that it naturally overflows to the people around me. I want to be like You. I want to love like You. I want to give like You. Bring to my mind the ways that I can stretch myself beyond the ordinary.

Amen.

CHAPTER 18: SUPERADDED MEMORY

GRIEVING WITH OTHERS

"If some have cause to celebrate, join in the celebration. And if others are weeping, join in that as well." Romans 12:15 (VOICE)

Many of us have days of the calendar year that are difficult for us.

An anniversary of a loss in our family.

A holiday that reminds us of something we don't have.

An event that reminds us of a painful time each time we hear about it.

With each date can come a sense of feeling very alone. No one else may remember that date of ours. After all, it's *our* hard date. It's *our* difficult holiday. It's *our* painful event.

Doesn't it feel refreshing when someone remembers our dates? Our heartbreaks? Our losses?

Don't we feel so noticed when someone—as this verse in Romans puts in—joins in on our weeping?

It's so comforting when someone says, "I remember what this date is for you… I miss him too."

It's so healing when someone goes out of their way to say, "I know this month is difficult every year. I am sad with you."

In order for us to give this going-out-of-our-way, healing kindness to others, we will need to choose to have a superadded memory—to remember our friends and loved-ones' "days."

Thankfully, for those of us who struggle with our long-term memory, we now have cool calendars and incredible technology to help remind us. We might not be able to remember *every* single date for *each* of our friends, but we can remember to write it in our calendar so we'll see it when that day comes. We can put the time into setting a reminder on our phone for the week before. When a holiday comes around, we can stop and think of who it might be difficult for and reach out to them.

We can make the decision to be intentional and *join in* with those whom we care for the most, on the dates that are especially meaningful to them.

In my calendar, I have a friend whose day is January 7th.
I have a friend whose day is Mother's Day.
I have a friend whose month is all of December.
Those dates have become my dates.

I know the sadness of having hard dates. And I know the joy when someone joins in on mine.

Don't we want to give others the joy of not feeling alone?

"He comes alongside us when we go through hard times,

and before you know it, he brings us alongside someone else who is going through hard times so that we can be there for that person just as God was there for us. We have plenty of hard times that come from following the Messiah, but no more so than the good times of his healing comfort—we get a full measure of that, too." 2 Corinthians 1: 4-5 (MSG)

We may have many losses. But this verse says we will have *more* good times than bad because of His healing comfort. And this same comfort He gives us—a superadded comfort, a full measure of healing—we are to give to others.

QUESTIONS

WHO ARE YOUR FRIENDS THAT HAVE IMPORTANT DATES?

WHAT TOOLS CAN YOU USE TO REMEMBER THOSE DATES BETTER AND MAKE THEM YOUR OWN?

PRAYER

God, help me live a life giving more good moments than bad to the world around me—by joining in on other's sufferings—like You have done for me. I want to care about what others are feeling. I want a superadded memory.

Amen.

CHAPTER 19: SUPERADDED BUDGET

SAVING UP FOR THOSE SUPER BLESSINGS

If we are going to super-add onto our lives the things that bring us joy, bring us towards community, bring us more filling routines, and bless other people, we will need to budget for the things that matter most.

For many of us, we can't just decide to add on trips to see our old college buddies once a week (even if they bring us joy), re-decorate our whole house (even if these new paint colors bring you more peace), or take a spontaneous vacation overseas with your spouse this weekend (even though that would be above and beyond, superadded, all the abundance and probably very holy). For most of us, we are going to need to assess what is the most valuable, the most filling, and the most beneficial for our unique souls and budget accordingly.

This will certainly take some subtraction, but the goal is to have funds for the right kinds of addition. When we subtract the things that we don't value, the mindless purchases that deplete our budgets, we are able to intentionally use those funds towards the things that truly and uniquely super-add onto our lives.

Proverbs 21:5 says, **"The plans of the diligent lead surely**

to abundance, but everyone who is hasty comes only to poverty." (ESV)

The Bible tells us that if we plan carefully and work hard towards our goals, it will lead to *abundance*— one of our favorite words. But if we are too quick to make our decisions it leads to *poverty*, our goals being set back, and a lack of resources when there becomes something we need or are passionate about.

What are things that you are passionate about? What fills you up the most? What are you making a priority?

One thing I am passionate about is being intentional with my long-distance relationships. My closest friends are scattered around the country and one thing that's always been important to me is having the resources to regularly see them or be there for any last-minute emergencies—a sickness in the family, a break-up, funerals, etc. There's a superadded budget for this. There are many things that are of less value to me that I don't spend money on, and that allows me to keep this as an utmost priority.

Another thing I prioritize is our outdoor patio. My husband and I work long hours and we love sitting outside on our patio together at the ends of our work days. We have made this space a main priority. It's filled with beautiful growing plants, strings of shining outdoor lights, colorful pillows and pots, and is a serene spot for the two of us. My husband also loves to grill and I love to garden so this space allows us to enjoy two things we highly value. Not all of the rooms in our house get this same kind of treatment, and there are things that we still want to improve inside the house, but we have subtracted some luxuries in other rooms to be able to super-add onto our homey patio, our peaceful garden, our little Heaven on Earth.

This practice embodies so much of what it means to live a superadded life—honestly assessing what is good for you and what isn't, what fills you up and what doesn't, and sacrificing the small things to place higher value on the big things. Intentional subtraction is a means to an end—a beautiful addition that fills your soul and increases the joy in your life.

QUESTIONS

WHAT ARE THINGS THAT YOU VALUE, THAT YOU WOULD NEED TO BUDGET FOR?

WHAT ARE THINGS THAT YOU VALUE FAR LESS THAT YOU COULD CUT OUT OF YOUR BUDGET?

WHAT WOULD IT LOOK LIKE TO HAVE A SUPERADDED BUDGET?

PRAYER

God, help me be wise with my money. I want to have more money for things that fill up my soul and not waste my resources on things that don't matter as much. Please show me the ways I can budget for some extra fun, some extra joy, and some extra passions. Bring to mind ways I can budget better and more intentionally.

Amen.

CHAPTER 20: SUPERADDED REALITY

"Let your adornment be what's inside—*the real you*, the lasting beauty of a gracious and quiet spirit, in which God delights." 1 Peter 3:4 (VOICE)

It can be easy to look like we have a balanced, rested, satisfying life.

It can be easy to curate an image of who we want others to think we are.

It can, at times, be easier to fake habits than make habits, fake community than make community, and fake a healthy soul than make the time to truly work on one.

But Jesus did not come to give us a superadded Instagram feed. He came to give us an actual, behind-the-scenes, in-person, real and tangible abundant *life*.

If we are going to spend time on anything—don't we want to fill the souls we really have? Don't we want to make the most of this one, beautiful life we have? Don't we want to pour our energy into something real that will last?

"Don't waste your time on useless work, mere busywork, the barren pursuits of darkness. Expose these things for the sham they are. It's a scandal when people waste their lives

on things they must do in the darkness where no one will see. Rip the cover off those frauds and see how attractive they look in the light of Christ." Ephesians 5:11-13 (MSG)

Continued in verse verses 15a and 16:

"So be careful how you live; *be mindful of your steps...* Make the most of every *living and breathing* moment because these are evil times." (VOICE)

Let us spend our days super-adding onto our *reality*.

Let us spend our days aspiring to be a person we are *proud of*.

Let us take no part in darkness or things that must be hidden.

Let us not waste our time obsessing over a fake reality.

Let us be careful with this sacred life given to us by God and mindful of every action we take.

Let us make **"the most of every *living and breathing* moment,"** and put our time, our energy, and our heart and soul into **"the real [us], the lasting beauty of a gracious and quiet spirit, in which God delights."**

Let us be intentional with the real person we wake up as and the real person we go to bed as.

Let us make the reality of our lives, *super*.

QUESTIONS

WHY DO PEOPLE SOMETIMES SPEND MORE TIME ON THEIR IMAGE THAN THE PERSON THEY ACTUALLY ARE?

WHAT IS ONE TIME OR ONE WAY THAT YOU HAVE BEEN GUILTY OF THAT?

WHY IS OUR TRUE SOUL AND TRUE LIFE SO MUCH MORE IMPORTANT THAN THE FAÇADE WE SHOW TO OTHERS?

HOW WOULD THE WORLD BE DIFFERENT IF EVERYONE COMMITTED TO SUPER-ADDING THEIR REALITY?

PRAYER

God, I want an abundant life. Not the appearance of an abundant life, not the reputation of an abundant life, but an actual abundant life filled, overflowing, and pouring over with Your goodness and joy. Reveal to me the ways I can super-add into my quiet moments, the moments no one else sees. Reveal to me the ways that I can keep improving. I want all You have for me, the real me. May my **"adornment be what's inside."**

Amen.

CHAPTER 21: SUPERADDED FOCUS

BOLDLY RUNNING TOWARDS MORE

"I've got my eye on the goal, where God is beckoning us onward—to Jesus. I'm off and running, and I'm not turning back. So let's keep focused on that goal, those of us who want everything God has for us. If any of you have something else in mind, something less than total commitment, God will clear your blurred vision—you'll see it yet! Now that we're on the right track, let's stay on it. Stick with me, friends. Keep track of those you see running this same course, headed for this same goal. There are many out there taking other paths, choosing other goals, and trying to get you to go along with them. I've warned you of them many times; sadly, I'm having to do it again. All they want is easy street. They hate Christ's Cross. But easy street is a dead-end street. Those who live there make their bellies their gods; belches are their praise; all they can think of is their appetites. But there's far more to life for us. We're citizens of high heaven! We're waiting the arrival of the Savior, the Master, Jesus Christ, who will transform our earthy bodies into glorious bodies like his own. He'll make us beautiful and whole with the same powerful skill by which he is putting everything as it should be, under and around him." Philippians 3:14-21 (MSG)

Wow.

"There's far more to life for us..."

I love those words so much.

There's far more to life than worshipping our selfish appetites.

There's far more to life than obsessing over our image and social status.

There's far more to life than researching what the world deems successful and curating our own version of it.

We are citizens, residents, and rightful dwellers of a place far better than the world we are worshipping.

Why are we aiming for anything less than Jesus? Why are focusing on **"something else... something less"**? Why are we running along this easy street—do we not see its dead-ends?

The writer here, Paul, beckons **"those of us who want everything God has for us"**—hey that's us!—to **"keep focused on that goal,"** the prize, the ultimate reward. That reward? It is our Savior, our Warrior, He who transforms us and renews us with all of His power, wonder, and might, He who fills our lives with an abundance of good things, He who adds, and adds, and adds some more.

If we want a superadded life, we need to super-add our focus. We need to reignite our determination. We need to boldly remember and act upon our goal. Let us stop negotiating with the values of the world. Let us stop making excuses for our earthly prides. Let us cease and desist in settling for less.

Perissos is ahead.

Perissos is what Jesus came to bring us—up from our home in Heaven, down to our temporary home here on Earth.

Through Jesus, there is a *perissos* life in store for us—a life far greater than what we have settled for.

Let's stay focused and keep running towards the goal.

There's far more to life for us...

QUESTIONS

WHAT ARE GOALS THAT THE WORLD HAS THAT ARE "LESS" THAN THE GOALS GOD WANTS FOR YOU?

WHY CAN IT SOMETIMES BE DIFFICULT TO STAY FOCUSED ON OUR ULTIMATE GOAL AND EASY TO GET DISTRACTED WITH OTHER PATHS, ATTITUDES, AND AMBITIONS?

WHAT ARE THINGS YOU HAVE BEEN FOCUSED ON THAT YOU DON'T WANT TO TAKE YOUR TIME AND ENERGY ANYMORE?

WHAT IS AN AREA OF YOUR LIFE THAT YOU HAVE LOST FOCUS IN WHERE YOU WANT TO BOLDLY REALIGN YOUR FOCUS, DETERMINATION, AND DIRECTION?

PRAYER

God, I want everything you have for me. Help me realign my focus. I'm sorry for the times I get distracted with the world's goals. I don't want to worship what it tells me to worship. I want my focus back. Show me the habits, routines, and attitudes I need to change, and help me boldly carry out new habits.

Amen.

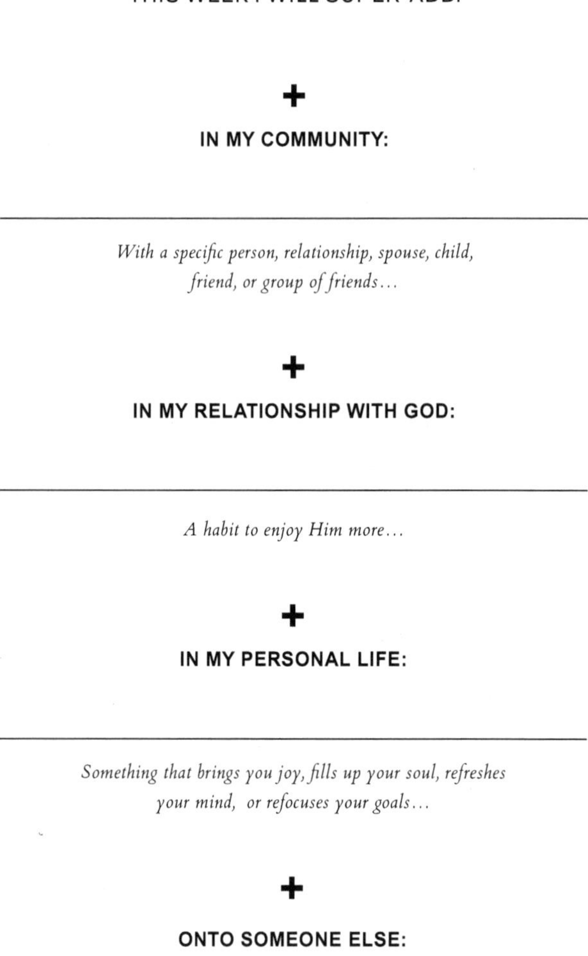

MY SUPERADDED LIFE

THIS WEEK I WILL SUPER-ADD:

+

IN MY COMMUNITY:

With a specific person, relationship, spouse, child, friend, or group of friends…

+

IN MY RELATIONSHIP WITH GOD:

A habit to enjoy Him more…

+

IN MY PERSONAL LIFE:

Something that brings you joy, fills up your soul, refreshes your mind, or refocuses your goals…

+

ONTO SOMEONE ELSE:

A way to super-add onto someone else's life…

I’
SE
FO

M DONE
TTLING
R LESS

PART  FOUR

CHAPTER 22: SUPERADDED MERCIES & SUPERADDED FAITHFULNESS

HIS MERCIES—THEY ARE ALL NEW, ALL THE TIME

"God's loyal love couldn't have run out, his merciful love couldn't have dried up. They're created new every morning. How great your faithfulness! I'm sticking with God (I say it over and over). He's all I've got left."
Lamentations 3:22-24 (MSG)

Sometimes it feels like I've used up all the grace God can give me. It feels some days that He has given me chance after chance, that I've said prayer after prayer, and that I'm a broken record asking for Him to show up in my circumstances over and over again. Every now and then I feel like I need to save some of these requests so He doesn't get overwhelmed with me, so His patience doesn't run out. In those moments, I just give

Him the burdens that are of the highest level of importance.

I love this verse because it reminds me that His love and compassion have no limits.

It reminds me that there is not a jar of God's mercy and love and forgiveness that I am dipping into, the levels getting lower and lower every time I come to Him.

It reminds me that I am the Limiter in this relationship. I've been limiting what God can do. I've been limiting what God wants to do. I've been limiting how much He wants to hear from me, give to me, and bless me with.

But God is not limited, nor limiting. This verse is a breath of fresh air to my exhausting assumptions, reminding me that His love and mercy is **new** every morning, He has **more** to give us each day, and He is **beyond** interested in and trustworthy with every detail, question, and worry in my life. He was faithful yesterday. He is faithful today. He will be faithful tomorrow. And the love and the mercy He has for me then will be new.

Growing up, I heard it said many times, "Put your trust in God!" And I'll be transparent and tell you that those words meant very little to me. They felt a little cliché and sort of went over my head—until I understood *why*.

Now I have seen the *why* in my own life.

My reality is this: Even at my worst He has never given up on me.

In my doubt. In my worry. In my constant back-and- forth. In my limitations. In my giving up. In my hopelessness.

He is persistent. He is limitless. He is faithful.

Every day, He wants to super-add His love, His mercy, His grace, His compassion, His healing power, His unending understanding, and all His wonderful goodness into our circumstances.

So, I have made the decision to trust Him with all of me.

I am declaring loudly with my life the same words as the writer of Lamentations: **"I am sticking with God!"**

I am super-adding my trust to a God whose faithfulness is never-ending but instead renewing, overflowing, and super-adding onto my life.

QUESTIONS

+

WHAT IS A WORRY, A QUESTION, OR A SITUATION THAT YOU CAN SURRENDER TO GOD AND TRUST HIM WITH TODAY?

WHAT WOULD IT BE LIKE TO TAKE YOUR LIMITS OFF OF GOD AND SEE HIS MERCY AND LOVE AS LIMITLESS?

WHAT IS A SITUATION IN YOUR LIFE THAT AT ONE TIME FELT HOPELESS, BUT GOD WAS FAITHFUL AND SHOWED UP IN WAYS YOU NEVER IMAGINED?

PRAYER

God, great is Your faithfulness. I want to trust You with every detail, every hurt, every question, every hope, and every dream in my life. I believe that Your love never runs out. I believe Your power is limitless. And I believe Your mercy, every day, is new. I trust You more than I trust my circumstances. I'm sticking with You.

Amen.

CHAPTER 23: SUPERADDED GRACE

"Today I am who I am because of God's grace, and *I have made sure that* the grace He offered me has not been wasted. I have worked harder, *longer, and smarter* than all the rest; but *I realize* it is not me—it is God's grace with me *that has made the difference.*" 1 Corinthians 15:10 (VOICE)

A super-added life does not mean a life super-adding work, check-lists, or regulations in order to earn God's grace, love, or approval.

The King James Version translates that verse in 1 Corinthians like this: **"I laboured more abundantly than they all: yet not I, but the grace of God which was with me."**

We read the term "abundantly" here once again, but this verse is referring to excessive labor, and the writer, Paul, is acknowledging that that's **not** what life is about, and that's **not** why he is who he is.

The same goes for us. Super-adding *labor* is not how we live our lives in the abundant, excessive, *perissos* way Jesus came for us to live.

"For it's by God's grace that you have been saved. You receive it through faith. It was not *our plan* or our effort. It

is God's gift, *pure and simple.* You didn't earn it, *not one of us did,* so don't go around bragging *that you must have done something amazing.*" Ephesians 2:8-9 (VOICE)

Let us not search for an abundant life through an abundance of impressive actions, legalistic requirements or moral codes, or the suffocating pressure of perfectionism. Does that sound like the superadded life Jesus came to give us? Not *even* close.

He came to give us an abundance of freedom through His abundant grace. We don't get to boast about this as if we've earned it. But we do get to enjoy it. We do get to celebrate it. We do get to live our lives in the freedom that through our faith in Him, we get all of His amazing, life-giving, and wonderful grace.

It doesn't take a life of working **"harder, *longer, and smarter.*"** We can't achieve it.

It takes a life of choosing to put our faith and hope and trust in Him. It's a gift. We receive it through faith, ***"pure and simple."***

Not only do we need to learn how to accept God's grace for us, we also need to super-add grace onto ourselves.

God gives us much compassion, so much freedom and understanding, but some of us have trouble receiving it and giving that same grace to ourselves. We can quickly feel like failures when we don't meet our own expectations. We can let missed deadlines or failed projects completely rule over our emotions and views of ourselves and others. We can attach our confidence and self-worth to our productivity, the things we work **"harder, *longer, and smarter*"** to be successful at.

And yet, God doesn't.

Why do we struggle so much with giving ourselves grace?

Why do we put more pressure on ourselves than God does?

Why do we assume that we somehow have the power to cause the world to end, the sky to fall, and our whole purpose, value, and calling to come crashing to the ground?

Do we not believe God can carry us? Comfort us? Redeem us? Rebuild us? And help us start again?

Do we not know the power and freedom in His grace?

Have we not fully accepted that it is not our works but only His grace ***"that has made the difference"***?

We can never say we ***"must have done something amazing"*** because all that we are is because of grace.

This truth lightens our load.

This truth sets us free.

It wasn't too long ago where I had a project fail, and I had to decide how to proceed with other upcoming projects. It was an overwhelming time, and I could see the stress of it all beginning to take over my emotions and confidence. I had to choose to super-add some grace onto myself. I had to say to myself, "I'm a flawed human, who works hard, with integrity, and God knows how hard I try."

I came to God with all the honesty, pride, and fear within me. I surrendered the stress I had put on myself and I prayed that He would take these burdens from me and carry me through. I received His grace. I cut myself some slack. I moved back deadlines. I canceled a couple of projects. I started a few new ones. And you know what? I was okay. The world wasn't ending. His grace was still enough. And I was still enough.

Let's subtract some pressure from ourselves.

Let's add some grace onto ourselves.

Let's receive His over-the-top, abundant, excessive, and overflowing grace into our lives and grab ahold of this superadded freedom.

QUESTIONS

WHY IS IT SOMETIMES HARD TO RECEIVE GOD'S GRACE?

WHY IS IT SOMETIMES HARD TO GIVE OURSELVES GRACE?

WHY DO WE SOMETIMES FEEL LIKE WE HAVE TO EARN GOD'S LOVE, SALVATION, OR APPROVAL?

WHAT ARE CIRCUMSTANCES IN OUR LIVES RIGHT NOW WHERE WE NEED THE FREEDOM OF HIS GRACE?

WHAT WOULD IT LOOK LIKE TO LIVE A LIFE WITH GOD'S GRACE ALWAYS AT THE FOREFRONT OF OUR MINDS AND SITUATIONS?

PRAYER

God, I receive Your superadded grace over my life and over my circumstances. I don't want to live in a constant state of fear or worry. I don't want to feel like I am carrying the burdens of the world all the time. I want to access, embrace, and receive the freedom of Your grace. Help me to super-add grace onto myself and to those around me. Reveal to me how wonderful Your grace truly is. I'm excited and anticipating grabbing ahold of this freedom.

Amen.

CHAPTER 24: SUPERADDED SAFETY & SUPERADDED FEARLESSNESS

"You, Eternal One, are my sustenance
and my *life-giving* cup.
In that cup, You hold my future and my eternal riches.
My home is surrounded in beauty;
You have gifted me with *abundance and* a rich legacy.
I will bless the Eternal, whose wise teaching
orchestrates my days and centers my mind at night.
He is ever present with me;
at all times He goes before me.
I will not live in fear *or abandon my calling*
because He stands at my right hand.
This is a good life—my heart is glad, my soul is full of joy,
and my body is at rest.
Who could want for more?
You will not abandon me to experience death and the grave

or leave me to rot alone.
***Instead*, You direct me on the path**
that leads to a *beautiful* life.
As I walk with You, the pleasures are never-ending,
and I know true joy *and contentment*." Psalm 16:5-11
(VOICE)

I love how this passage sings of God's abundance, shouts of God's provisions, and declares the safety we have in Him.

He holds our future.

He surrounds us with beauty.

He gifts us with abundance.

He orchestrates our days.

He is present—He is here, right now in this moment.

He goes before us. He stands beside us.

He doesn't abandon us. He directs us.

Life with Him is **"a good life… a beautiful life."**

He gives gladness to our hearts, joy to our souls, and rest to our bodies.

As we walk with Him, we know **"true joy *and contentment*,"** and the pleasures are never-ending, over-flowing, above and beyond what is necessary.

With God, we rest in superadded safety.

Our hearts, our minds, and our souls are in the hands of

a protective, gracious, abundantly giving, always-loving, fighting-for-us God.

"Here is the bottom line: do not worry about your life. Don't worry about what you will eat or what you will drink. Don't worry about how you clothe your body. Living is about more than merely eating, and the body is about more than dressing up.

Look at the birds in the sky. They do not store food for winter. ***They don't plant gardens.*** **They do not sow or reap—and yet, they are always fed because your heavenly Father feeds them. And you are even more precious to Him than a beautiful bird.** ***If He looks after them, of course He will look after you.***

Worrying does not do any good; **who here can claim to add even an hour to his life by worrying?**

So do not consume yourselves with questions: What will we eat? What will we drink? What will we wear? Outsiders make themselves frantic over such questions; ***they don't realize that*** **your heavenly Father knows exactly what you need. Seek first the kingdom of God and His righteousness, and then all these things will be given to you too. So do not worry about tomorrow. Let tomorrow worry about itself.**

Living faithfully is a large enough task for today." Matthew 6:25-27, 31-34 (VOICE)

With God, we can subtract our worry.

We can surrender our fears and our anxieties.

Through our worrying, the Enemy steals our joy, our security, and our trust in God. He subtracts hours of our lives through worry. This verse says to, instead, seek God's kingdom first, put aside anxieties about the future, and *just live faithfully today.*

Let us not allow the Enemy to have victory over emotions. Let us walk boldly in the truth that we are safe in the hands of our loving God.

"Because the Lord, the Eternal, helps me
I will not be disgraced;
so, I set my face like a rock, confident
that I will not be ashamed.
My hero who sets things right is near.
Who would dare to challenge me?
Let's stand *and debate this* head-to-head!
Who would dare to accuse me? Let him come near."
Isaiah 50:7-8 (VOICE)

Because of God's superadded safety, we can subtract our worry, and, instead, super-add our fearlessness. We can super-add our confidence that we **"will not be disgraced."** We can super-add our boldness that we **"will not be ashamed."**

Our Hero, our Champion, our Warrior—He fights for us, He protects us, and He stands alongside of us through all the battles of our lives.

When we embrace this truth—what do we have to be afraid of?

When we live in this certainty—what power can the Enemy have over us?

Let us rest in God's overwhelming safety. Let us stand up to the voices of fear and worry. Let us set our **"face like a rock"**—unwavering, undeterred, and unafraid. Let us add up, pile on, overflow—and approach each and every day—with *fearlessness.*

QUESTIONS

WHAT ARE THINGS THAT BRING YOU WORRY?

WHAT ARE FEARS AND ANXIETIES THAT THE ENEMY USES TO STEAL OUR TRUST IN GOD?

WHAT DO THESE THREE PASSAGES, IN PSALM 16, MATTHEW 6, AND ISAIAH 50 REVEAL TO YOU ABOUT THE NATURE OF GOD'S PROVISION AND HIS ABUNDANCE OF SAFETY?

WHAT ARE THINGS YOU WANT TO SURRENDER TO GOD TODAY? WHAT WORRIES DO YOU WANT TO SUBTRACT FROM YOUR LIFE?

WHAT IS AN AREA IN YOUR LIFE THAT YOU WANT TO WALK IN WITH SUPERADDED FEARLESSNESS?

PRAYER

I

Pray a prayer of thanksgiving to God for His safety and provision. Pray a prayer surrendering to God the things that the Enemy uses to cause you worry, stress, and fear. Pray a prayer asking for God to reignite your boldness, confidence, and fearlessness.

In the name of Jesus. *Amen.*

SUPER EXTRA

++

RE-READ THESE VERSES:

PSALM 16:5-11. MATTHEW 6:25-27, 31-34. ISAIAH 50:7-8.

WHAT STICKS OUT TO YOU? WHAT GIVES YOU HOPE? WHAT'S AN IDEA OR PHRASE FROM THESE VERSES THAT CAN BECOME A MANTRA FOR YOU THIS WEEK?

CHAPTER 25: SUPERADDED STAMINA

STAYING POWER. ENDURANCE. GRIT.

"...We instructed you how to live in order to please God, as in fact you are living. Now we ask you and urge you in the Lord Jesus to do this more and more." 1 Thessalonians 4:1 (NIV)

As we grow closer to the end of this book, we are nowhere near done exploring this superadded life.

There is so much more to discover. There is so much more that God wants to add onto our lives and into our relationships with Him and with others. There is so much that He wants to reveal to you, specifically, and in your own circumstances that I did not/will not/could not possibly cover in this book. This book is 28 chapters. Let's be real. This barely scratches the surface. There is *so much more* that God has in store for *you*.

Don't stop digging deeper now.

Don't stop living in His abundance now.

"Do this more and more."

In this verse, Paul is encouraging his friends in Thessalonica in a way that I need encouragement some days, and right now—I want to encourage you.

Keep loving those around you well.

Keep subtracting the negatives in your life.

Keep adding on all the good things God has for you.

Keeping creating moments to read His Word, speak to Him, and worship Him.

Keep living a life of thankfulness.

Keep living a life of heavenly interruptions.

Keep finding new ways to rest in and enjoy God's presence.

Keep seeking ways to trust Him like a child.

Keep exercising self-control when it's hard, forgiving offenders when it seems impossible, apologizing when you're wrong, giving above and beyond, and going out of your way to be extraordinary.

Super-add that love.

Super-add that perspective.

Super-add that freedom.

Honestly assess how you can do better in the areas of your life that need work. Everyone's strengths and weakness are different. Once you know what yours are, super-add your energy and time into improving on those areas, little by little, step by step, addition by addition. It may take some time, but don't worry—God is *super* patient. Don't give up on grabbing ahold of all God has for you.

He knows how hard we try. He knows how much we give.

That's sort of a scary thought, because He also knows when we're putting Him and the life He has for us on the back-burner. But more than anything, it's freeing. It's freeing to know that God knows when we're giving all we got, and He is honored and loved by that.

Giving our *honest best* honors God.

The Voice translation of 1 Thessalonians 4:1 put it this way: **"Live a life that is pleasing to God as you are already doing. Yes, we urge you to keep living and thriving in that life!"**

Don't back down now. Don't get tired now.

Super-add your stamina. Stretch your staying power.

Keep up your endurance. Reignite your grit.

Keep living and *thriving* in this life of abundance.

QUESTIONS

HOW WILL YOU CONTINUE TO CHALLENGE YOURSELF IN LIVING A SUPERADDED LIFE?

WHAT ARE HABITS YOU WILL BEGIN OR CONTINUE AFTER FINISHING THIS BOOK TO ALLOW GOD TO KEEP ADDING ON *ALL* HE HAS FOR YOU?

WHAT WOULD YOUR LIFE LOOK LIKE IF YOU KEPT YOUR COMMITMENT TO THESE PRACTICES?

PRAYER

God, give me a new energy, a fresh wind, and an even greater desire to access all You have for me. Help me remember all You've taught me, and more than that, don't stop teaching me. I want to know You more. I want to receive more from You. I don't want to give up now. I want to keep thriving. I want *more* and *more*.

Amen.

CHAPTER 26: SUPERADDED FAMILY & SUPERADDED WEAPONS

**"Father to the fatherless, defender of widows—
this is God, whose dwelling is holy.
God places the lonely in families;
he sets the prisoners free and gives them joy."** Psalm 68:5-6a (NLT)

For some of us, the idea of *family* is difficult. There has been some subtraction, some division, some hurts, and some loss for us.

The Enemy has stolen, killed, and destroyed some hope for us.

God wants to heal those broken pieces of our hearts. He wants to occupy those vacancies. He wants to fill those gaps—to place **"the lonely in families,"** set us free, and fill us, *overflow* us with joy. He desires each of us to have a safe community that is layers deeper than surface-level friendships, a resting place for our souls, a home that we know we are always a part of no matter what.

God explains what He wants to do and how He is going to do it in Zachariah 9:12-13.

"I announce today that I will restore to you twice as much as what was taken. For My people will be My weapons." (VOICE)

God doesn't just want us to survive our family circumstances. He doesn't want us to just make it through a life of emptiness. He wants to restore unto us **"twice as much as what was taken,"** above and beyond what we lost, and exceedingly more than what was stolen from us. He wants us to have a superadded family—a family that is over the top and excessive in safety, love, and joy.

How is God going to do that?

His *people* will be His *weapons.*

God is declaring war on the brokenness of our hearts, our families, and our homes, and He is using *His people* in order to do so.

Through men of God, He is providing fathers.

Through women of God, He is providing mothers.

Through the family of God, through His Church, God is providing mentors, teachers, big sisters and brothers, best friends, companions, husbands, wives, sons, and daughters—God wants to add onto our lives a family that is far larger than we could have ever imagined.

Ephesians 2:19 says, **"You are no longer called outcasts and wanderers but citizens with God's people, members of God's holy family, and residents of His household."** (VOICE)

One amazing thing about being a child of God is that we are

not the only one. There are many children, many people that God wants to pour out His goodness upon, many people that Jesus came to give abundant life to, and many people that God wants to heal, renew, and restore.

And we are the weapons for one another.

We are how God is going to restore to His other children twice as much as what was stolen from them.

Not only will God use His people to do a miracle in our lives, but He also wants to use us to be the miracle in someone else's life.

1 Corinthians 12:27 says, **"You are the body of the Anointed, *the Liberating King*; each and every one of you is a *vital* member."** (VOICE)

God wants to super-add onto our lives, and He wants us to super-add onto others. We are a vital member of this family. We are an important part of this body. We are the battle plan. We are His weapons.

For some of us, we need to be intentional in seeking out members of the family of God and asking them to join us on our journey. When we find these people, we'll need to be brave enough to be vulnerable. It's not easy to reach out. It's not easy to open up. But through His people, God wants to surround the lonely with families, He wants to restore unto us far more than what was taken, and He wants to abundantly add onto our lives a community that is far deeper and wider than we have ever hoped for. I hope you pursue and embrace God's superadded family into your life.

For others of us, we need to be aware of those who may need to be surrounded. Perhaps we are the family that can super-add onto their lives. Who around us needs a mentor? Who is someone that has nowhere to go for the holidays? Who are people that we can pour God's love onto, invite into our communities, and be the weapon God wants to use so that He can reclaim and rebuild their lives? It won't be easy for them to reach out. It won't be easy for them to open up. But we are *vital members* of this family. And just as someone once added onto our lives, we too can bring God's beautiful addition to someone else.

If we are all intentional in these two areas, there's no telling how superadded, excessive, over the top, and abundant this family is going to be...

QUESTIONS

WHAT DO YOU THINK OF WHEN YOU THINK OF FAMILY?

WHAT DO YOU THINK OF WHEN YOU THINK OF THE FAMILY OF GOD?

WHO IS SOMEONE IN YOUR LIFE THAT EITHER HAS BEEN YOUR SUPERADDED FAMILY OR YOU HAVE SUPER-ADDED FAMILY ONTO THEM?

HOW CAN YOU BE INTENTIONAL WITH REACHING OUT TO PEOPLE AND ADDING THEM INTO YOUR COMMUNITY AND YOUR FAMILY?

WHAT WOULD IT LOOK LIKE TO LIVE YOUR LIFE CONSTANTLY ADDING ONTO THIS FAMILY?

PRAYER

I

God, I want a superadded family.
Restore unto me twice as what was taken from me.
Fill in the empty parts of my life. Bring miracles,
bring weapons, bring Your family to come and
surround me. And help me see how I can be that for
others. Help be aware of those in need around me.
I want to super-add onto this family as well.

Amen.

CHAPTER 27: SUPERADDED GOAL

MORE LOVE, MORE LOVE, MORE LOVE...

"Go after a life of love as if your life depended on it—because it does." I Corinthians 14:1 (MSG)

What does our life need to be filled up with more than anything? We know God wants to super-add rest, joy, grace, and family into our lives. But what addition is the most important? What, at the end of the day, *is* a superadded life?

A life of love.

In the NLT, 1 Corinthians 14:1 is translated:

"Let love be your highest goal!"

More than any of our other goals, even some of our good goals—our ambitions of being successful, having friends, getting that job—this verse is saying that *love* is the ultimate goal. Love must be a higher, more important, and greater goal than any other. We must live our lives—and live out our dreams—with this being our main focus at all times.

Ephesians 5:1-2 says, **"Watch what God does, and then you do it, like children who learn proper behavior from their parents. Mostly what God does is love you. Keep**

company with him and learn a life of love. Observe how Christ loved us. His love was not cautious but extravagant. He didn't love in order to get something from us but to give everything of himself to us. Love like that." (MSG)

Jesus came to give us an *abundant* life.
He came and loved us with an *extravagant* love.
What God mostly does is just *love us and love us and love us*, and *give to us and give to us.*
He loves and gives in order to add *all of Himself* into our lives.

When we receive Him, draw near to Him, speak to Him, and read His words, we learn what living this same kind of *life of love* looks like.

It is a superadded life.

And...

It is a super-*adding* life.

The same love that has so fiercely and fully filled us, God wants it to overflow out of our lives and fill those around us.

We don't even have to wonder what this is like.
1 Corinthians 13:4–8a describes exactly what a life superadded with love looks like:

"Love never gives up.
Love cares more for others than for self.
Love doesn't want what it doesn't have.
Love doesn't strut,
Doesn't have a swelled head,
Doesn't force itself on others,

Isn't always 'me first,'
Doesn't fly off the handle,
Doesn't keep score of the sins of others,
Doesn't revel when others grovel,
Takes pleasure in the flowering of truth,
Puts up with anything,
Trusts God always,
Always looks for the best,
Never looks back,
But keeps going to the end.
Love never dies." (MSG)

When we are living with love as our highest and ultimate goal, we are living with superadded patience, overflowing kindness and selflessness, super-subtracted jealousy and grudges, excessive forgiveness and humility, abundant truth, abounding trust and hope, pouring-over positivity, and superadded endurance.

When we live our lives consumed with God's love, we also receive (typical of always-adding-God) something else pretty amazing.

1 John 4:17-18 says, **"God is love. When we take up permanent residence in a life of love, we live in God and God lives in us. This way, love has the run of the house, becomes at home and mature in us, so that we're free of worry on Judgment Day—our standing in the world is identical with Christ's. There is no room in love for fear. Well-formed love banishes fear. Since fear is crippling, a fearful life—fear of death, fear of judgment—is one not yet fully formed in love."** (MSG)

A life filled with love is a life without fear.

Fear and love can't exist together—**"a fearful life...is one**

not yet fully formed in love."

God's love subtracts, demolishes, and casts out our fears, our worries, and our anxieties.

This love is the most freeing, amazing, world-rocking gift of all.

This love is the highest goal.

This love is the most important thing to be filled with.

This fear-destroying, burden-releasing, shame-killing love is the same love God wants to pour *into* our lives and then let it overflow *out* of us onto the world *through* us.

Let us **"go after a life of love as if [our lives] depended on it."**

Let's show the world a God, a love, and life that is over the top, above and beyond, excessive, and superadded.

Let's partner with God in banishing fear.

Let's live lives constantly speaking, abundantly giving, and super-adding love.

QUESTIONS

HOW WOULD SOME OF OUR GOALS, MOTIVES, OR AMBITIONS CHANGE, IF LOVE WAS AT THE ROOT OF THEM?

WHAT IS ONE THINGS THAT AMAZES YOU ABOUT GOD'S LOVE?

IN 1 CORINTHIANS 13:4-8, WE READ ABOUT THE CHARACTERISTICS OF LOVE. WHAT IS ONE CHARACTERISTIC THAT YOU WANT TO IMPROVE IN AND SUPER-ADD INTO YOUR LIFE? WHAT IS ONE THAT COULD OVERFLOW MORE INTO THE LIVES OF THOSE AROUND YOU?

WHAT IS A FEAR IN YOUR LIFE THAT YOU WANT GOD'S LOVE TO CAST OUT?

WHAT ARE FEARS THAT THE PEOPLE AROUND YOU MIGHT HAVE THAT YOU COULD HELP SUBTRACT BY OVERWHELMING THEM WITH LOVE?

PRAYER

God, I want love to be my absolute highest goal. Help me to see the ways I can super-add love to the world around me. May love be the root of my ambitions. May love be the center of my agendas. Reveal to me the ways that I am currently not speaking or acting in love, and help me discover how to honestly improve in those areas. I want to live without fear. I want to grab ahold of this superadded goal.

Amen.

SUPER EXTRA

++

LET'S BE SUPER PATIENT WITH PEOPLE THIS WEEK.
LET'S BE SUPER KIND. LET'S BE EXCESSIVELY POSITIVE.

LET'S LET GO OF A BUNCH OF ENVY, PRIDE, AND LISTS
WE HAVE OF WHAT PEOPLE HAVE DONE OR OWE US.
LET'S CHEER FOR OTHERS ABOVE AND BEYOND
WHAT IS NECESSARY.

LET'S HAVE MORE TRUST, MORE HOPE, AND MORE
ENDURANCE THAN WE EVER THOUGHT POSSIBLE.
LET'S HAVE LOVE BE A LITTLE EXTRA IN OUR
LIVES THIS WEEK.

CHAPTER 28: A SUPER-ADDING GOD

WITH SUPERADDED LOVE + POWER

"*Father*, out of Your *honorable* and glorious riches, strengthen Your people. Fill their souls with the power of Your Spirit so that through faith the Anointed One will reside in their hearts.

May love be *the rich soil* where their lives take root. May it be the bedrock where their lives are founded *so that together* with all of Your people they will have the power to understand that the love of the Anointed is infinitely long, wide, high, and deep, surpassing everything anyone previously experienced.

God, may Your fullness flood through their entire beings.

Now to the God who can do so many *awe-inspiring things, immeasurable things*, things greater than we ever could ask or imagine through the power at work in us, to Him be all glory in the church and in Jesus the Anointed from this generation to the next, forever and ever. Amen." Ephesians 3:16-21 (VOICE)

We are able to live superadded lives because of a super-adding God.

He adds to us more than we have asked for, beyond what we have prayed for, and over the top from what we have imagined.

The love of Jesus is so superadded, we can't even comprehend its massiveness. The MSG translation describes it as **"the extravagant dimensions of Christ's love. Reach out and experience the breadth! Test its length! Plumb the depths! Rise to the heights! Live full lives, full in the fullness of God."**

The **exact same word** used in John 10:10 to describe our lives—"abundant," perissos, is used here to describe what God does through His power in us: **"exceeding abundantly above all that we ask or think."** (KJV)

That. Is. Incredible.

An excessively amazing, dimension-defying, world-rocking God, with massive love and crazy power is able to—**with that same power**—do *abundantly* more through us than we can comprehend.

A superadded life is then not just filled with all of the fun, joy, and rest and all of life's extravagant toppings—which are all Biblical and wonderful—but also(!), the superadded life Jesus came to give us is overflowing with power and wonder and with the abundant love and power of God at work deep *within* us.

When we give our lives fully over to God, when we decide to walk with Jesus for the rest of our days, and when we invite the power of His Spirit to live inside of us, we do not only live an outwardly abundant life, but we also have something superadded within us. Something the Enemy can't take away. Something no man can subtract. Something the world can't snatch.

Though the Enemy has come to steal, kill, and destroy, Jesus came to give us that *perissos* kind of life, **with** a *perissos* kind of love, **from** a *perissos* kind of God, with a *perissos* power through a *perissos* Spirit, doing *perissos* work within us, around us, and through us.

All He has already done—He wants to do **more**.

All we are asking—He wants to give us **more**.

All we think He is and can do—He is and will do **more**.

More than we need. Above and beyond what is necessary.

Excessive.

Superadded.

That is the life Jesus came to give us.

This is the life He died for us to have.

That is the life we have access to when we receive Him, put our trust in Him, and live for Him.

A superadded life—inside and out, now and forever—from a super-adding God.

Life abundant.

No less.

QUESTIONS

HOW DOES KNOWING THAT A SUPER-ADDING GOD, WITH SUPERADDED POWER AND LOVE, SENT HIS SON JESUS TO GIVE US A SUPERADDED LIFE, FILLED WITH THAT SAME POWER AND LOVE, CHANGE HOW YOU THINK OF GOD AND HOW YOU THINK OF YOUR LIFE?

IF THERE WAS ONE MAIN THING YOU TOOK AWAY FROM THIS BOOK—THIS IDEA OF EMBRACING A SUPERADDED LIFE—WHAT WAS IT?

PRAYER

I

God, I want to live an abundant life, no less. Help me to continuously discover what that means, and how that looks in my day-to-day life. I don't want to settle for anything less than all that you have for me. Thank you for all of it.

Amen.

MY SUPERADDED LIFE

THIS WEEK I WILL SUPER-ADD:

IN MY COMMUNITY:

With a specific person, relationship, spouse, child, friend, or group of friends...

IN MY RELATIONSHIP WITH GOD:

A habit to enjoy Him more...

IN MY PERSONAL LIFE:

Something that brings you joy, fills up your soul, refreshes your mind, or refocuses your goals...

ONTO SOMEONE ELSE:

A way to super-add onto someone else's life...

EPHESIANS 3:20 (VOICE)

"NOW TO
WHO CAN
AWE-INSPIRING
IMMEASURABLE
THINGS
EVER COULD
THROUGH THE
AT WORK

THE GOD
DO SO MANY
THINGS,
THINGS,
GREATER THAN WE
ASK OR IMAGINE
POWER
IN US."

EPHESIANS 3:20 (VOICE)

NOTES

1 — Strong, James. *Strong's Exhaustive Concordance of the Bible*. Abingdon Press, 1890. http://biblehub.com/greek/4053.htm

2 — Helps Word-studies, copyright 1987, 2011 by Helps Ministries, Inc. http://biblehub.com/greek/4352.htm

3 — Thayer, Joseph Henry. *The New Thayer's Greek-English Lexicon of the New Testament, with Index*. Lafayette: Book Publ., 1981. http://biblehub.com/greek/4053.htm

SUPER THANKS TO—

CHRIS AND RACHEL. I COULDN'T HAVE DONE IT WITHOUT YOU. YOU OPENED THE DOOR FOR ME. YOU DA BOMB.

SEAN, SHELLEY, ALLISON, KATE, AND EMILY. YOU FOUGHT FOR ME, STAYED WITH ME, YOU'RE AS WEIRD AS ME, AND I LOVE YOU GUYS.

MY MOM, LIZ, AND MY BROTHER, ELIJAH. YOU ARE EVERYTHING TO ME. THANK YOU FOR BELIEVING IN ME. I LOVE YOU BOTH SO VERY MUCH.

MY HUSBAND, GUY. YOU'RE THE MAN. I'M AMAZED BY YOUR STRENGTH, COMPASSION, AND PERSEVERANCE EVERY DAY. THANK YOU FOR HOW MUCH YOU LOVE ME, HOW MUCH YOU FIGHT FOR ME, AND HOW MUCH FUN YOU ADD ON TO OUR LIVES IN THE SIMPLEST, MOST WONDERFUL WAYS. I LOVE YOU WITH ALL OF MY HEART.

YOU HAVE EACH ADDED ON TO MY LIFE MORE THAN YOU KNOW. THANK YOU ALL FOR BEING MY SUPERADDED TEAM. I LOVE BEING ON YOURS.

Natalie
Kasey
Bethany
Lori
Karrie
Elaine
Ali
Lindsey
Nicole
Laura
Lindsay
Shauna
Allison
Rachel
John
Cheryl
Johnny
Jeni
Mac
Mary
Marnie
Jessica
Rick
Kay
Josiah
Mario
Julianna
Jud
Mike
Lisa
Amber
Danielle
Nick
Drew
Jake

Tim
Tiffany
Darryl
Tracy
Jenny
Kyle
Ben
Bec
Greg
Lori
Mark
Juby
Jonathan
Elyse
Jazzy
Xavier
Jose
Samantha
Natalie
Cora
Danny
Niall
Bryant
Sam
Ally
Kelly
Allison
Taylor
Heather
Todd
Patty
Tim
Jessica
Michael
Brandi

Lisa
David
Heather
Raul
Kevin
Patriece
Dustin
Jacqui
Beau
Evan
Garrett
Matt
Bill
Sue
Samantha
Lance
Candace
Adonis
Mark
Christie
Derek
Lisa
Holly
Charlotte
Mikey
Eric
Socrates
Jyro
David
Amber
Trisha
Shua
Andy
Jason
Ed

Dennis
Sandy
Big Jim
Rob
Connie
Nin Nin
Michael
Javier
Stefanie
Tiffany
Lisa
Joe
Mallory
Maureen
Stephanie
Sara
Gabriel
Candy
Pam
Natalie
Whitney
Bryan
Gary
Lindsay
Bryce
Laura
Kenny
Marla
Darin
Ryan
Jack
Kayla
Jordon
Andraea
Rob

MANY PEOPLE HAVE SUPER-ADDED ONTO MY LIFE. THANK YOU. +

ABOUT THE AUTHOR

Hosanna Wong is a writer, speaker, and spoken word artist who shares stories of freedom and hope to various ages, cultures, and communities around the country. Known for sharing complex Biblical truths through simple, raw, and captivating stories and refreshingly accessible applications, Hosanna speaks and performs at churches, conferences, prisons, and various urban ministries year-round. Under the name Hosanna Poetry, she has released two spoken word albums and is the author of *I Have a New Name*. *Superadded* is her second book. A San Francisco native, Hosanna and her husband, Guy, are currently based in Los Angeles, CA.